SIX WOMEN IN A CELL

SIX WOMEN
IN A CELL

A Story of Sisterhood and Survival
After Police Assault

DIANA TOKAJI

Publisher's Cataloging-in-Publication Data

Names: Tokaji, Diana, author.
Title: Six women in a cell : a story of sisterhood and survival after police assault / Diana Tokaji.
Description: Includes bibliographic references. | Silver Spring, MD: Root to Rise Productions, 2020.
Identifiers: LCCN: 2020919390 | ISBN: 978-1-7341485-1-0 (pbk.) | 978-1-7341485-2-7 (ebook)
Subjects: LCSH Tokaji, Diana. | Women--Crimes against. | Psychic trauma. | Post-traumatic stress disorder. | Police--United States. | Women prisoners. | | BISAC BIOGRAPHY & AUTOBIOGRAPHY / Women | BIOGRAPHY & AUTOBIOGRAPHY / Social Activists | BIOGRAPHY & AUTOBIOGRAPHY / Personal Memoirs
Classification: LCC HV6250.4.W65 .T65 2020 | DDC 362.83/092 --dc23

First Edition, 2020

Book design by C'est Beau Designs

To the Reader

Each person will receive this book according to
how the abuses of power in our society and our world
have impacted her directly—or how they have not.

It is my duty to tell this story as it unfolded.

I have tried to do so here with accurate recall
and without harm.
Some names have been altered.

To Betty

WHO LISTENED, FEARLESSLY.

CONTENTS

Your silence will not protect you.

—AUDRE LORDE

INTRODUCTION

THE WOMEN STOOD IN A jagged circle in my deadened brain. No one else would ever know they had gathered; that they could tell my story.

We were raw. Naked.

Transparent.

We were strangers, yet we knew how to stand in presence, how to move in toward the other or back out.

The night was long; shock had numbed us; our contact was random—two of us, five of us, three. Conversations took seconds. And I will never see them again, there is no way to just "stay in touch." They remain like the weird halo after a flashbulb—the *dzzz* image hanging in smoky air, hooked there, demanding witness. I'd be surprised to go back to the cell and see we are gone.

Each woman entrusted me with a piece of her story. Later I found that by telling theirs first, I could manage to dive in again, write my own. But barely. It is written, yes—the manuscript has been complete for years. But releasing it in book form has been a whole other kettle of fish. Six years after the police assault, I am wondering if it still isn't better to wait another decade or two, stuff it in a drawer, stall 'til I'm dead. Because I don't want to give that bully energy another day, another second, of my life. I want it to go away. *I want to make it go away.*

I work with assault survivors now, women with stories that make mine pale. They forever wish their ordeals would disappear, un-happen. Like an expunged criminal charge—*poof*, to be

1

cleared—*you're good to go.* I, too, want to get on with the last chapter of my life, want to write and dance and counsel and fight for goodness.

There is a "but" here.

But good prevails? *But* time heals everything?

But what is toughest may hold the greatest teaching, stretching us so beyond capacity that we transform and our suffering compels us into action to help others?

No:

But I can still be taken down.

Another young man shot. Another woman harmed. That raw, desperate place—I know there is no "recovery" for them: Lives change forever at these moments, even when the victim survives. From health and breath patterns to executive function and relationships—everything is altered. I survived, and this is how. Not prettily; not bravely; not romantically; and obviously not without price, given that I am still scared to publish this.

Am I afraid that when this becomes public I might be hurt in some way? I am afraid. Am I afraid of retaliation? My dreams say yes. Afraid of being judged? Of wanting to reach out through the stratosphere and correct any misinterpretation? I am afraid. I am very, very, constantly afraid.

But I am afraid of my alley too. And of night. And of police on duty—what if one stops me for a missing brake light—what reaction might surface in me, what suspicious trembling and incoherence as I fumble for my license, innocent but for the rage I harbor? Older; white; woman: the least profiled—yet I am duly scared, for myself, and for others. For kids playing with toy guns. For hooded teens. For a Black professor strolling animatedly *in her own affluent neighborhood.*

For mothers, whose grown kids will be on their own when roughed by cops. For Black men walking at night.

Or day.

For cops...who also have bodies.

Fear is not a deterrent. The pen insists: plant one in every bag and by bedside, in car and kitchen. Take one for a walk. Scrawl the lines across the page, vomit the story—guts up—and with that blue Pilot pen, file the fucking words. There's no choice really; my body becomes unwell unless I own what happened. The pen is a truthteller.

It was Hallowe'en night. For we six women in the cell it was a most memorable, tricked-out Hallowe'en. We were in a concrete box and had suffered a mean road to get there. Surely, the treat, dear Baby, dear Alexa, dear Richmond, dear Social Worker, and dear oh dear Mudd, is the memory of your faces still gnawed into my mind. And your stories, spare and intimate, that propelled me to write *this*.

Diana Tokaji
November 2014 to August 2020
Silver Spring, Maryland
U.S.A.

CHAPTER 1

Baby

———

Mutism is so addictive. And I don't think its powers ever go away [...] it's always there saying, "You can always come back to me. You have nothing to do—just stop talking."

—MAYA ANGELOU

BABY

WHEN I FIRST SEE BABY *everything stops. She seems to have frozen in the middle of the cell, her feet so planted, if her eyelids didn't blink I'd think she was standing dead.*

She's not like Alexa, who makes everything move. Alexa is water; she bubbles. She fills out the tan prison jumpsuit to perfection. Her black hair is French-braided and tied with toilet paper—after all, our hair clips and rubber bands were confiscated. Alexa tells her pain story while laughing, and though it looks like any moment her smile could flip, it is laughing that's Alexa's mainstay.

Baby is the opposite—dead serious. Even as she tells me her story, the only sign of life is in her eyes. They are brown eyes and huge as if yanked wide beyond her freckled face, their mad largeness alone keeping her upright. Each time Baby blinks, it is startling—even breathing is a risk—how tempting to crack, curl to our own feet and bawl. I never learned her name, but I learned this:

Baby, an eighteen-year-old senior in high school, who is at most five feet tall and shaped soft and round, was bullied by another girl and that girl's friends. Something mean was put on Facebook; something mean spread around the school. They'd threatened her at the bus stop and cornered her in the hall. Baby had had it and when she finally took a hand to her bully, in her words:

"That slap on her face felt so good, once I started I couldn't stop."

Two days later, the bully was in the hospital and three police officers were at Baby's door.

The urge comes over me to cross the cell and hold Baby, let her cry against my own shaking chest. But I know better—I have two teens. Besides, we haven't met; I was simply slammed into the same cell, my long grey hair disheveled, my yoga pants dirt-stained from where the cops knocked me down on the corner of our lot. That was just an hour ago, and although I could easily be Baby's grandmother, I am hardly reliable material for a hug.

I give her the most hope-filled expression I can muster, although all I want to do is swear. I'm angry at everything that congealed to make Baby victim to a nasty girl's hate: Had her parents cared? Did anyone have her back? Had she been totally alone with the daily assaults on her ego, her two inches of self-worth? Hurt begat poison, poison/rage, rage/ violence—such an obvious, ancient equation.

"I'm so sorry this happened," I say to Baby. I do not say the words "to you." Just: "this happened," this escalation, with Baby in the hot seat. Now she is standing so still, I don't dare say more. Her future is yet to unfold, some of it dependent on the bully in the hospital and how well she recovers. Baby will be called to The Commissioner in a few minutes: it's midnight, she's been here since morning.

Time stops.

The air hangs.

We stand in the cold cell seeing each other.

Our breath hunkers down to a hibernator's low and no one's ribs move. If we are still, none of this has happened, and the glaring fluorescents don't buzz with spite. We're just surprised square dance partners catty-corner to each other, frozen under the same absence of sky.

I don't ask her any more questions. I don't try to strategize and I don't probe. Baby's owl eyes are tortured enough. I simply hope now—and pray later—she takes my face and keeps it.

"NOW IT'S YOUR TURN," she said. She was a smart one, Baby, and she wanted my story. Maybe she'd already figured me out, the way I listen a lot, to bodies and hearts. Baby looked at me with suspicion, perhaps wondering why I, age sixty, stood open-mouthed and tongue-tied when she'd articulated her own drama in quick sound bites: surely I could produce the same. She was on to me, that kid.

But even as a two-year-old, speech wasn't my medium and my parents wondered if I was "slow" because of it. Back then they used the word "retarded," and they asked the doctor if I was. Uncle Peter argued that I was smarter than all of them and would speak in my own time, but they suffered while I pointed to random food items from my high chair, grunting loudly, or if that didn't get what I wanted, barking like a walrus till they understood.

On one such occasion, the story goes, I barked one time too many and too loud. An adult threshold was reached and I still hadn't gotten what I wanted. One more bark did it and my mom, who died when I was six and other than this story is painted as a saint, picked up a can of Real Whip from the table and whip-creamed my face. I trust she shook the can first.

My ragged copy of *Gerald McBoing-Boing, The Noise-Making Boy*—an oversized children's fiction book about a boy who doesn't say words but makes sounds instead—is still on my shelf, and is so well-read that it barely maintains a spine. Gerald never grew out of his wordlessness, but this lack was eventually recognized as virtue, and he became a "clip-clop, boom-boom" sound-effects radio announcer, making millions for his proud parents. These words I write without pulling the book from the shelf, fifty-eight years later. Gerald is in my bones.

In addition to working as a yoga therapist, my other working life has been as a choreographer, performer, and as a writer—all non-verbal arts, though true enough I often use spoken word on stage. And my favorite language next to Spanish is American Sign Language, where words and body are one—a high contrast to us English-speakers, Monty Python-esque with only our lower jaws racketing up and down.

But Baby wanted words not gestures, and I had not yet told my story. For it wasn't a story yet, it was what only one hour, two hours ago happened, and no linear reduction of the experience had yet been acquired within me. Nor *required*. It would be soon though, that night or the next day or the next, when my turn with The Commissioner would be announced, and I'd be re-handcuffed, frisked facing the wall, and taken through the iron gates to sit outside his bulletproof window answering questions, my left wrist handcuffed to the desk so my right was free to sign documents. That would prove in itself a challenge due to the extent of trembling that pounded my limbs and the condition of the pen, hardly a pen at all. It was only the flaccid innards, the ink tube that's left when you've taken a pen apart: not only could it do no harm upon the armed guards surrounding me, but it could barely service a signature.

Baby was waiting for my response. I loved her then, if I didn't already love her for beating the shit out of that girl. I know I'm not supposed to say that, and these words won't get hours knocked off my Community Service, but I was already sick of the bully-girl's face and I'd never seen it. I steadied myself and looked hard at Baby.

Had kids cornered her because she wasn't skinny? And what of Baby's suffering had racist undertones? Fair-skinned and mixed-race, freckles matching her reddish-brown hair, springy and free, Baby might morph into a beauty of her own later, but now…now was she the butt of jokes from her peers because she was plump, red-haired, and fit no camp?

In a distant way, I too identified as "other", though I was perhaps only confused—or made mentally flexible—from three different mothers who sequentially raised me. My DNA was likely Russian and eastern European, yet at Baby's age when I was attending Berkeley High School in the era of Vietnam War protests and student power, I was often courted to join the Asian Student Union. I wasn't sure I had blood rights to this, though faint Mongolian traits from my first mother's genetics reflect around my eyes and cheekbones, and "Tokaji"—a Hungarian region and the name of a grape—is also a Japanese surname. At age twenty, when I waitressed at a Japanese restaurant, the cook asked through an interpreter if I'd drunk a lot of milk as a child. He wanted to know how a Japanese girl had grown so tall.

But somehow it was less this Asian link and more the bloodline of my second mother that embedded sweetly in me, and I was constantly surprised that I wasn't part Cherokee, part African, myself. Jimmie-Lee Caldwell had promised my dying mother—her close friend from the women's peace movement— that she would watch over my sisters and me, and over the next three years from age six to nine, my young body merged with hers, big as a man's, silken and spirit-strong. Her voice was melody, even when I wouldn't eat or when I'd read myself into a stupor. We shared a bed many nights, her long, generous arms hugging her son on the left and her "daughter Didi" on the right, we two children unaware of the loaded, poisonous charge of color.

Of course I didn't condone what Baby had done; someone was seriously hurt and someone was seriously going to pay for that. But I got it that Baby had been the brunt of a cocktail of prejudices, and her own sainthood had reached threshold. Like my first mom, she'd had no real answers from adults in how to deal with these bludgeoning noises coming at her. She whip-creamed that girl. Made the noise stop.

Baby and I stared at each other so long that in any other context one of us would have gone shy and flinched away, turning our gaze somewhere, anywhere, to break the intensity. We'd just met, there was no obligation to be or say anything to each other, not here in this concrete box. Was anyone else in the cell yet? If so, I have no memory. We were locked in the dance of our standing bodies, perhaps six feet from each other, so fully engaged that the space was a wash-out of everything but her. I wanted to tell Baby my story as clearly as she'd told me hers: *this; then this; pause; then that.* In the pause the whole story comes down like the sky emptying snow after a build-up. Everyone gets it.

But my snow was still building and I wasn't sure how to dump it. I was shaking with chills while my ears and cheeks blazed swollen and burned like frostbite. My lips were stuck to my gums, my mouth dehydrated so that the usual slip 'n' slide of lips over teeth—such a simple, constant function requiring no effort, no attention—was, to my distress, not happening. I had to unhook my lips with my fingers to speak; between words the inner lips stuck on the dry sand that was my mouth.

Perhaps it was in part being face down in the dirt while wrestled into handcuffs that had done it. Perhaps it was shock, the relentless layering effect of violations, first of our home, second to my body, third because whisked by squad car to God knows where.

"God knows where" is where I was now, no longer a mom with a professional identity, but a criminal with a mugshot, thumb- and finger-printed, some miles anywhere north and west of my home in a freezing cell where available water was either toilet water or bathroom sink, about which a guard, when questioned, said, "Yes, I'd drink from it, if I had to."

Perhaps it was all of the above that was screwing with my thermostat, as well as fresh fear from what I held in my right hand, a paper copy of the charges against me—including the statement a cellmate would later read to me, that I had assaulted four police officers. Three additional criminal charges were listed, one of them "resisting arrest," so baffling in that I'd never heard them state such, nor did I understand, at any point, their violence to my body as *arrest*. My maximum sentence was inscribed under the charges: *thirteen years in jail.*

Salivation and lacrimation are healthy functions—and mine were on strike. Every blink soon became a slice 'n' dice, my contact lenses wrecking my eyelids from lack of lubrication. Perhaps I was better off for this fight-or-flight inhibitory response: had I the ability to cry right then, I might have sobbed so hard they'd tranquilize me.

Instead, my face was a raging desert and my body was freezing, blinded in the blur of lost eyesight. When they took me out of the cell to re-fingerprint me due to a blurry first set, the guard had difficulty stabilizing my trembling thumb. I mentioned that I felt ill. He said, not unkindly, he could call the prison nurse. I was afraid they would take my blood pressure, which might be through the roof, or check my pre-diabetic blood sugar and find it whack, then force me into some procedure. Later, my cellmate, Mudd, as ever in an advisory, mentorship role to me though perhaps forty years younger, told me I'd made a smart choice to refuse the guard's offer to call Medical. "Never trust what they might do," she said.

But my body's involuntary behavior felt explosively out of control: I could combust, implode, heat or freeze to the point of permanent damage. More storms were coming and I couldn't even find the words to describe to Baby how they'd first started.

I was making hot cocoa. I knew that. It wasn't rich enough so I was doctoring it with dark chocolate powder and then balancing that with sugar. I was using half milk and half water but it didn't seem creamy enough so I added some beautiful cream from the local farmer's market.

Is this my story?

This is not the story Baby wants, nor what The Commissioner will want. But it is my story.

My stomach hurt. Maybe from testing the cocoa. Maybe because I was hungry. Maybe because I'd also tested the Hallowe'en candy. Or because the day had been full with demands. I'd seen a client to make up for a session she'd missed. Last minute grocery shopping was next at several stores, Bundt cakes picked up for the party, candles for pumpkins, more marshmallows 'cause someone ate the bag I'd just bought. I had pumpkins to carve and was the only one who'd do it. I always made a carving decoration, just letting the knife express the pumpkin. I had a house to clean and a ghost to hang—ritually constructed from an old bed sheet and black construction paper for eyes. Like my cellmate Alexa, I take my Hallowe'en seriously.

My younger son's college applications were due that night and he'd been trying to finish the essay for the University of British Columbia in Vancouver before his backyard party. There'd been last-minute proof-reading for me, and last-minute costume consultations. Our older son, Daniel, was already in the northwest—we'd encouraged both boys to branch away from the Washington, D.C. area. It was worth tonight's push to get the UBC application in by the 8:00 p.m. deadline.

Down the block, sangria was served for neighbors and for parents accompanying trick-or-treaters, and several folks had asked me to come. "I have to man the door," I'd said. I was adamant about acknowledging each kid's costume, whereas the guys in my family just hand out the candy and go back to reading their Kindles. I actually love Hallowe'en. Or loved it.

My stomach hurt from the confluence of tensions and candy and this was what I wanted to tell Baby. But I knew it didn't matter to the story, or to her, or The Commissioner. It was my sensory truth, however, and this is my overpowering brush to paint with. For my sensory is everything. It's how I feel my way through the day, how I make decisions, how I choose fruit at the store. My stomach doesn't typically hurt, but it hurt then. Did it know something was coming? Did it need food? I lowered the cocoa to a slow simmer and marinated some tofu. I steamed broccoli. I sat down and ate. Maybe my stomach would feel better.

I stood up again and was stirring the cocoa, quite perfect now, deep and dark and rich but not too rich. I would serve the kids just after my husband, Robin, served the BBQ chicken. He was on the deck directly above the yard, a nice cool night with no wind so the kids could sit around the fire. I'd made the fire pit with leftover slate a neighbor had discarded after building a stone wall. I'd carried those stones to my car and then from my car, with Mikey's help, to this far point in the yard, just for moments like this one: teens around a fire pit hanging out.

Several kids were on the trampoline, chatting and softly bouncing, two others bobbing up and down getting a free ride.

Several others were in hammocks in the gazebo we'd built. The gazebo was my favorite place for a yoga practice when weather permitted.

It was at this tranquil moment—I wanted to tell Baby—as I was stirring the perfect hot cocoa at the stove, that Yaya ran in through the open back door, breaking the hum. She was screaming in a high soprano, raced past me in the kitchen and then began twirling in place like a cornered mouse.

"Oh my God! Oh my God!! Oh my GOD!!!"

Her hands were fingertips in mouth playing the keys of her teeth, twiddling there frantically; she turned and turned in tiny steps, her tall frame bowed over, her panicked cry: "Oh my God I'm so scared Oh my God Oh my God. CAN I GO HOME?" she begged, stopping her twirling for a moment.

Of course, I thought, dumbfounded. She could go home anytime she wanted; *Why would she even ask me this?*

I had known Yaya since Ms. Well's kindergarten class. Her mom was outspoken in the PTA and her brother, Elijah, an amazing saxophonist at a young age, created his own music to accompany me at my Fringe Festival performances. We'd won Pick of the Fringe awards together. I'd known Yaya since she was five, holding her mom's hand as they got off the ride-on bus and crossed with the crossing guard to our elementary school, her mom in high heels that would have broken my feet.

But I hadn't seen Yaya in at least two formative years, and she was probably eighteen now. I'd run into her once where I teach at Strathmore Center for Music and the Performing Arts. I was substituting on a Sunday and saw Yaya through the Levine Music School's glass window, singing a solo in front of Tony Award-winner Sutton Foster and an audience of wannabes. Hers is a talented family. This tall, mouse-spinning version of Yaya was therefore familiar, but I wasn't certain.

"Yaya?" I asked cautiously at first, and seeing her recognition of me, I continued. Of course, I realized at that moment, I had changed at least as much as she had. My red-brown hair, once super short and then pixie and chin length, was now grey and long. Surely she was confirming who I was as much as I was confirming that this was indeed a chiseled and elongated version of the girl I'd watched grow up.

"Police were here!" she blurted out.

"Okaaaay," I said. It seemed that was supposed to explain something, but it just opened the sentence to an unfinished end. "What did they want?" I asked.

"I don't knooooow," she wailed, returning to panic, her eyes back to cornered mouse.

"Can I go upstairs?" she begged suddenly, as oddly and desperately as when she'd asked if she could go home. The attic steps we'd carved out of a small closet in the dining area led upstairs to my combo study, bedroom, yoga space, the loft where I did all my work and saw clients. It was a shoe-free zone.

"No, I don't want people upstairs," I said, then wondered why she wanted to hide. "Did you do something wrong, Yaya?"

"No."

"Then why do you want to go upstairs?"

"Because I'm so scaaared!" And then came a resurgence of tears and the wail: "Can I PLEASE go home?"

"Of course you can go home," I said, now a touch annoyed. *It's a free country.* "Are the police still here?" I asked, returning to problem-solving parent mode.

"No."

"Then why are you scared?"

"Because they were SO scary."

"They came into the backyard and then they left, right?" I said, to confirm the information.

"Yes!"

"Then why was it scary?"

"Because they TOOK SOME KIDS Oh my God Oh my God Oh my God," she cried out in one long exclamatory run-on.

"They *took some kids*, Yaya???" I asked, incredulous.

"Yes and they were so scary Oh my God."

By now, to confuse the issue—and how will I explain this in any linear way to Baby and the other cellmates who will want my story, and how on earth will I state it to The Commissioner: for this is what it all turned on, the entrance of seven unannounced police into my yard, the taking of kids from our barbecue, and the hysterical teens dashing through my kitchen—at the same time as this conversation with Yaya, in ran two senior high school males, one looking like he'd seen a ghost, pop-eyed and frantic, the other holding a wet paper towel to his brow, bending over to re-position it, then running for the bathroom, not hard to find, there being but one bathroom in this small bungalow...*Did the police hurt this boy...why was he holding his forehead?*

"The police were here!" said the uninjured teen.

"Did they hurt your friend???"

What was going on here would someone please tell me what happened to our idyllic scene? Lila, an incredible party-planning teen, had grocery-shopped earlier with Mikey—bags of ice, chicken, hot dogs, veggie burgers, buns—and other teens had arrived with fold-out tables, sodas, snacks, plastic cutlery, tablecloths. Together we'd run an extension cord and hung a work light from an umbrella to light the food table, an improvement over the original solution, a dangling cell phone with a flashlight app. We'd resurrected the mini Christmas lights scalloping the gazebo, creating a magical fairyland effect. It was our first party in how long? Since their middle school years, the time when everything is supposed to turn sour, and hormones and teen angst run high, but instead, their middle school years had been heaven, socially. Seventeen middle school teens had carried the trampoline from several blocks away where a neighbor was done with it ruining her grass. They'd lifted it over our six-foot fence and spent many after-school hours on it. High school had turned more serious, and less backyard hangout time had been happening, until tonight.

The boy's injured brow turned out to be unrelated to police, though it took minutes to understand that. He had been on the trampoline and his forehead intersected with another bouncer's cell phone. The police had not hurt this kid. Okay. But the police had removed several kids from our party?

I grabbed a jacket and raced down the stairs. It was thin polar fleece. Blue. The gentle grey-blue of a seal. Are seals grey-blue? It was bought five years ago at REI. On sale. The sleeves do that thing where they hook around your thumb and keep your wrists warm. I really like that when I'm walking the dog.

This is not the story Baby wants. She wants the part where there are police and I have somehow ended up in jail. But I cannot make sense of that story yet, have no arrangement of thought that makes sense to me, let alone language to tell it. My sensory hasn't caught up to real time. This is walrus-barking material, Gerald McBoing-Boing stuff, this is the muteness of shock and freezing fear. I call to my brain for a straight line of information, but find grey and black film stuff, relentlessly fast-paced, confusing, film noir storms. There will be multiple, battering storms still to come: The Commissioner, a lawyer, the court, the sergeant detectives—I will have to machete through menacing clouds for language and I will have to start now.

Baby's owl-eyes are demanding of me: *Whoo? What?* When Baby asks me again, out of a sense of obligation to return the respect of her story for mine, I say all I can that makes sense to my body, my crazily vibrating body, my lips-stuck-to-my-gums-in-the-middle-of-the-night-in-a-cell-somewhere—not at all clear to me where—body.

I manage two sentences for Baby, which, for now, will have to do:

"I was making hot cocoa," I say. "I was stirring it."

INTERMEZZO 1

Dreams
Nightmares
Visions

———

JOURNAL

October 25. (6 days before assault and arrest)
I feel so much vitality in my body.

November 18. (17 days later)
I am fighting for my life.

December 22. 2 a.m.
I am scared of how angry I am
— how my mind
revisits each scene.
In a dream I am

    Taking
    Back
    My Alley

and cops come.

I want to blind them
with my high beam flashlight
as they did.

I am screaming:

If you TOUCH ME
I will scratch-scrape-bite-howl
until you kill me.

January 11.
I am numb to January.
I am numb to just turned
January.
I am numb.

February 6.
Children come in to the
Gated yard just as I'm
Trying to get out and
Away from the crocodile.
I am trying to get the
Kids to come out before
The crocodile jumps them
& there's one more kid
& one more. It's
Shaking my insides &
Making me convulse
To get them out in
Time. My urgent
Gut-ripping cries
Wake Robin.

The main thing is
The kids walk out
Of the yard single file
SINGLE FILE!
They are so slow because
They've been trained to be
Obedient – but a crocodile
Is behind them!

March 20.

Snow falling on first day of spring.

I begin to make amends with how little capacity to understand

among those outside of the ACLU folk.

Good to testify before the House Judiciary Committee in Annapolis.

To have voice and power.

For one minute and 59 seconds.

April 14.
Nightmares
& the whole day
carrying this pain around.
It is, I swear
the weight of
a tiny world.
I carry it
& want to
take it to my nest.

At the same time
I will be frank
I vomit it
I vomit this world
I vomit it again
& time again
all over the floor
the bucket the bowl
I vomit from the roof
so hard I will fall
fall into my vomit
down from the roof
and back to the blackness
of safety.

Nest of my heart
I will find you
like the arms
of a mother
reaching through everything
wretched stinky rancid
for her child.
Stench & puke & feces
she reaches for her baby
I will find you, she says searching
& she will:
Her baby waits
expecting it.

August 11. 3 a.m.

It has been ten months. I awake from nightmares and in the Washington Post article I read, it speaks of *rage* still burning a year later in Ferguson. I am nodding my head. The rage in me is staggering.

Rage, coursing through the daughter of a pacifist who devoted his short life to peace and justice.

Rage. Grounding yoga poses have kept me on earth when I wanted to flee. Restorative poses—*with my eyes open*—help now when my body is exhausted. But guess what else I've taken up? Boxing. And I will tell you frankly, I hit hard. And there is a face I see when I hit that bag.

Rage. The first moral principle of Yoga is *ahimsa*, non-harming. It is my credo. I am determined not to perpetuate harm. And yet, in the reflexes of my body, in the dark marrow of bones hurt and the moral injury to my soul, every ounce of cellular strength could rally and counter-attack they who harmed me—the police, the system, the mindset, the paralyzed politicians in the sack with the FOP.

Rage. The second moral principle of Yoga is *Satya*.

Truth.

I return to it when my rage frightens me; when I begin to cave into hopelessness. I return to what I know is true, what must be done, what should be known and said out loud. Looking out the window at my backyard on my 61st birthday on your protest anniversary, Ferguson, I ache for you. Speak the truth. Even the harsh truth of *rage*.

May it be heard.

CHAPTER 2

Alexa

———

The level of anger in this world is unhealthy. Chill.

—ALAN GROSS,
ONE YEAR AFTER HIS RELEASE
FROM PRISON IN CUBA

ALEXA

ALEXA WORE A PRISON JUMPSUIT well, having entered the detention center in a sweatshirt and her boyfriend's plaid boxers. I know this because I was with the guards doing my first set of thumbprints and mugshots when she entered the jail and passed me by, chatting and laughing as if she'd arrived in a spa.

Even later when the bitterness toward her ex came out, she had the kind of smile on her face of a singer reaching with hope and determination to a high note. She was happy but occasionally random in conversation, acting as if we'd been on a certain topic for a while when really all the dialogue had been within her head only. It was endearing though, and on Alexa not at all weird.

Any of us in the cell could have been nuts. There were no introductions to each other, just a loud clang and the sudden appearance of a new woman, arriving in whatever state her circumstances had borne. My grey hair was a mess and the front of my pants had soil from my backyard on them. My eyes popped out like a "Berkeley Crazy" I'm sure, a term that hails from my teens when, several years after moving from Ohio to California in time for the passage of Governor Reagan's Proposition 13 closing mental hospitals, I saw quite a few people on *our Berkeley streets turn aggressive in self-talk. "Those f-ing Russians are attacking Mars and I won't have it, I'm telling you, and I'm telling the goddamn president," one short, muscular woman ranted while stalking up and down the aisle of the #51 bus, searching for eye contact with some sucker she'd then scream at for looking at her. I rode that bus for forty-five minutes on Tuesdays and Thursdays to get to Grace Mann's Studio, where I swept the stairs in exchange for my first ballet classes. Scared of the "crazy lady" on the bus then, I wore her bug-eyed edginess now.*

But Alexa's scattered behavior was more Amelia Bedelia than Berkeley Crazy. Amelia Bedelia, as you might know, was the star of a children's book series, a sweet, happy-go-lucky character who simply interpreted things her own way. "Dust the furniture" she interpreted as sprinkle powder on the furniture. "Dress the turkey" she took to literal proportions—a Scottish vest and stirruped pants on the raw bird. Always smiling—flitting actually—she made major gaffes, yet the twinkle in her eyes never failed, whereas the rich woman who hired her was always in gloomy distress. This was Alexa, although it would turn out she had plenty to worry about. The twinkle never deserted her, and it was only her chatty style and her flitting around the cell that suggested a touch of crazy at a time of gravitas.

Unlike the #51 crazy who John-Wayne'd down the bus aisle in her neat khakis, I was not only disheveled, but was holding onto the walls to stand. No moment of repair with a sink, a comb, a mirror was in my future. I wanted to crouch low in front of the phone to see my reflection in the silver square at its base but was afraid I'd risk even more of a weirdo label. I tried to catch a glimpse of myself later as I passed a glass-framed notice on the wall while walking with the guard from my second round of thumbprints. Knowing it was important to act normal, I didn't stop there to primp, though I was desperate for my own reflection. Had I been able to see myself, it might have reassured me I was me.

Most of us—hunched over from the cold, and freaky-eyed as we anticipated the future—looked not so sane. We had no identifiers—no jewelry, no scarves or belts, jackets, sweaters, no shoes. Several of the women had come in without socks and had been assigned blue paper booties to wear on their feet. This, as you can imagine, dear reader— this je ne sais quoi splash of cheer, making it like Darwin delightedly coming upon a beach lined with Blue Footed Boobies—added not too much in the normalcy column, and bumped the surreal tally high. I hadn't realized just how much a woman reassures another woman of her sanity with the messages from a hair clip, or an earring that catches the color of her T-shirt.

Only Alexa presented in prison as if she'd had some prep time, perhaps with a beautician or color consultant. She entered through the slamming doors and hope blew in along with her picturesque black French braids laced white with the aforementioned toilet paper. A Latina Heidi, Alexa's lungs inflated as if to yodel from alpine heights, filling to perfection the bosom of her tan prison jumpsuit. And the cuffs that would have been floods on me, landed at her ankles like a tailor's hem. Her form was reassuringly starched next to my collapsing one—her hair shone, her spine was upright, head level and proud. Her smile alone was a miracle in this context, her brown eyes sparkling clear.

The only frailty Alexa showed, the only crack in her carefree manner, became apparent after we spoke for a while. It was the way she looked indirectly and not quite at me as if that let her stay in her own jolly world. It was a harmless, self-engaging non-eye contact, and it seemed to match the logic of her random comments. "It's funny," she said after a long silence, seemingly out of the blue and looking just to the right of my head, "I'm Puerto Rican, but my boyfriend, who is white, speaks better Spanish."

ALEXA HELPED ME WHILE WE were still strangers, when I grappled with the wall phone like an ape with a can opener. "Here, let me show you," she said. "You smash your ear into this hole to hear the directions, and then jog your mouth and shout into the lower hole." Even after pressing 1 and then 1 and then 3 and pause and then 3 and then area code and number, the connection cut off when the receiving party, my anxious husband, answered.

Her bounciness only lapsed when she napped on her back on the cement step that lined the cell wall. No one else slept, or even reclined. Freezing temperatures, blinding fluorescents, obnoxious loud television no one watched, the unknown of when the metal door would slam and the next name would be called, Alexa slept with apparent quality, turning off all sensory and going to enviable, healing privacy like a monk atop a mountain sitting deep in his *pratyahara*.

"Did you lead your cellmates in a yoga class?" a friend asked me a week following this night, verbalizing the romantic version I'm sure many people pictured. It was a valid question.

Had I been there for an ongoing time, I'm sure I'd have turned to my practices. But no, I did not lead my cellmates in a yoga class. "In fact," I told my friend, "I couldn't breathe."

I could not breathe. I am a yoga therapist and I couldn't breathe. Nor could I *try* to deeply breathe. Rather, I gasped for each breath. Gasped for the upper chest "accessory" breathing yoga therapy works to dissolve in the population who comes to us with compromised immune systems, cancer, inflammatory bowel disease, back pain.

Am I saying all illness stems from accessory breathing, the hyperventilation/over-breathing that is symptomatic of panic and sympathetic nervous system arousal? Well, yes… susceptibility to illness is linked to the chemistry that changes when our breath shifts out of balance due to tension patterns, stress, shock, trauma, fear.

High chest breathing signals chemicals for emergency adrenal response—which cranks up our respiratory rate further. It's a cycle. Though we feel like we don't have enough oxygen, and gasp for more, we're actually suffering from a lack of carbon dioxide and can't use the oxygen at hand. Ideally, we might re-balance by following the natural urge to *flee* the danger that's stressing us— we'd move or run to re-set the breath and chemistry. Or, we would reset by retaining an inhalation, then exhaling slowly, gradually increasing the length of each exhalation: Inhale for 5, hold for 3, exhale for 7.

If possible. None of this was possible. I was handcuffed and couldn't escape. I was jailed, so ditto. I was barely surviving, so marching in place or rhythmic breathing were not on my list. Two and three years later, I would still be working on my re-set button, and the consequences of adrenaline and cortisol overload would play out in my inflamed skin, loss of hair, and tremors. If instead of handcuffs and a jail cell, I had been bear-hugged by my husband or son for ten to fifteen minutes after the police assault, perhaps it would have been different.

Because a hug might have relaxed my diaphragm, the main breathing muscle. The diaphragm and the intercostals between the ribs generously contract, and in their motion rhythmically massage our viscera while increasing our lung capacity. They keep our interactive organ function fluid like neighbors who are friendly in their work together, even within the scrim of their own homes. These lyrical movements of deep breaths also take our vertebral column on a spacious ride of expansion and contraction, expansion and contraction. How good is that free ride, comforting like rocking a baby, sending an "A-OK" to our nervous system, and a "yay team" to homeostasis. Then the connective tissue that is our webbing, our elastic separation between organs, and our stretchy connection from brow to plantar fascia of foot, from hip to opposite shoulder like the diagonal sashes of a pageant queen, spirals and weaves, laughing through the body like Alexa in a jail cell: *I'm easy, I'm breathing, I'm expansive, all is well.*

True, I was older than Alexa by about thirty-five years. True, I'd just been kicked to the ground, violently handcuffed, threatened with tasing, insulted, blinded, and *then* escorted at high speed to the cell; whereas each of my mates was surprised by police in their home or car. Fair enough that I couldn't breathe, that I was beet red, my ears inflamed like an angry elephant, my body producing chemical output faster than a soda machine. No, I didn't do a single yoga pose in the cell and I didn't try to breathe at any point that night, nor for weeks after. It would be unabashed survival—mouse-sized sips of breath in, with almost no exhale out, and a friend who two days later with all good intentions said: "Just BREATHE!" nearly got the yoga therapist's knuckle special. I would learn this great lesson the hard way: *Do not tell an assault victim to breathe during the acute stage following trauma.*

The way Alexa walked in smiling without any pants as if arriving to jail in men's plaid boxers is an everyday affair, was cool. It was enviably cool that she could stay cool. But I, who on most occasions love parody, even slapstick, and can be brought to see the humor of a situation, saw now absolutely none. Although, I did have one fleeting moment of seeing the bizarre comedy within the horror story. It happened after the cops sat me up, handcuffed, seated on the corner of our lot.

"I'll bet you were drinking," said the most aggressive cop, who my husband would later say seemed like the alpha male gang leader of the seven. Had he spat on my face it would have had similar effect, as those words implied that I was in some way crazy to find it unusual for seven police to enter my backyard and remove teenagers from our party without consulting the adults.

"Don't come between a mother bear and her cub," my friend Carol would recite to me a few days later after I'd called her to come over—afraid as never before that I wouldn't live to crawl to the phone for her help. I was suffocating and choking on tears. I had tried to leave the house for my son's soccer game and fear had slammed me out of nowhere. I looked at her incredulously when she said that phrase. *Oh*, I thought. *Right.* My friend's words reminded me of the sane thing a parent does to protect her young: She goes to that young.

"Don't come between a mother bear and her cub," Carol repeated, shaking her head, as if this was the most obvious recipe of life that everyone knows. Did the police not notice this was our *home*, I am the *Mom*, these are our *sons*? Later I would understand this again and again when I heard panels of women, and when I was on a panel with women, whose sons had been killed by police. *This was my BABY*, they would say, if not in words, in the desperate look in their eyes.

But surely maternal instinct and a sense of responsibility for the teen party-goers weren't enough to cause me to take issue with the police aggression. From their perspective, my behavior was whack—I should have rolled with the punches that Friday evening when they swept into our yard. The police were investigating an assault that had occurred somewhere in our neighborhood, and they had their own reasons to suspect our teens. They were doing a job, they were in a hurry, and I was in the way. For a woman to insist on staying while the kids were questioned, choosing the responsibility of being a mom over her obedience to the police—surely that woman was either A) crazy, or B) drunk.

But this is supposed to be the singular humorous moment I am recapping for you, although to begin with, the story is not funny. For the cop's high-power flashlight blinded me square in the eyes as I sat handcuffed below him, and the haze of his body broke into shards behind the radiant beam. I shook my head, baffled not only that he would assume I was drunk, but by how I'd landed here.

With Yaya's last words, I'd run from the kitchen to the back gate, only to find the exit blocked by one male and two female cops.

"Go back inside," they'd said. Two of my son's closest friends were being questioned by an elderly, bald cop to my left; his eyes instantly registered to me as safe and sane. But the three cops blocking my way were hostile, their expressions aggressive, their body language forceful.

"I've known these kids since Kindergarten!" I exclaimed, as if that mattered.

"You can't be here," they said.

I explained that I was *the mom* in charge of this party—this was my home. Perhaps the police didn't know that. I was sure the women cops would understand.

And then, past their heads, I saw in the distance my own son, flanked by uniformed police in the dark end of the alley. It was like arriving to frozen tundra and when I turned north to breathe, only tundra, south, tundra, east and west ice and ice, endless, blue impermeable. *Mikey???* All I could make out in the dark distance were two beautiful eyes I knew.

My husband, to my left, stood in shock, as he too, saw for the first time our younger son in the night distance surrounded by cops.

"That's my son!" I said.

"You can't speak with him."

"Then I won't speak. I'll just stand near him," I said. And seeing one of the female cops pause and nod as if granting me permission, I set out walking toward him.

The blonde female cop stood in front of me. I moved past her. Someone shouted, "That's assault!" and suddenly two bodies jumped on my back.

"For crying out loud, I'm just walking to my son!" I cried, and continued hobbling toward him mindless of the two bodies.

Later, I experienced a most melancholy sense of joy hearing the videotape of myself saying those words. *For crying out loud* is not a phrase I ever say. Ever. But my father, born in 1924 and gone by 1983—far too early for the world he tried to protect—did indeed say those words. How did those words come out of me at that moment? Weeks later, I would reach for my father again, and for my mom who had died in her thirties, digging deep when isolation, grief, and darkness would take me where no one should go alone.

They wrestled me into handcuffs and sat me up. The alpha cop stood over me shining a high beam flashlight in my eyes. My son videotaped this, although at first when the tall, skinny cop guarding him said, "Put that away," my son had obeyed. But when they tackled me to the ground, he pulled his phone out again and instantly hit record.

"I have a right to do this," he said.

"You have a right to do a lot of things," said the skinny cop.

The video captures this dialogue as well as the wrestling match with me on the bottom. Then you see me manually seated upright, a forced audience to the bully cop's words, delivered as though I'm the dirt my face had just been in.

"I bet you've been drinking," he says.

And I am so incredulous I cannot speak. I forget my state, my handcuffed state, and the fact of multiple patrol cars with their lights doing that police car lightshow in circles dusting the night air and the trees and the cool autumn road. From cross-legged sitting, my handcuffed arms painfully wrenched behind me, I perform a slow untwirl to stand the way Marcia Singman taught us in modern dance class, Berkeley High School P.E. I am up in a flash and leaving—to go where? Even at this moment, kicked to the ground and forced into handcuffs, I clearly do not understand the game of cops and robbers. I am the bad guy they have just caught. I have been handcuffed "for crying out loud." I am not allowed to up and leave. This does not occur to me.

For the cop had spat a final insult that landed like a torturous hot drip on my psyche, and my system said *Flee!*

I'm out of here, said my obedient sixty-year-old body, and it twirled up from the ground, armless, to run.

"Mom! Mom!" I hear my son's voice and remember my surrendered status. I spiral back down to the ground as smoothly as I'd spiraled to rise, all of which I owe to Mrs. Singman, and none of which I paid a price for immediately. But like a whiplash victim, years later I still struggle walking down even a shallow flight of stairs, my knees remembering being knocked to the ground, remembering this no-hands standing up, this no-hands return to seat. My nervous system will also remember that I could not flee, that at this moment my son's counsel was the only option if I wanted to live.

"Oh my God," I say. I'm in disbelief that this bully would hold such low regard for a weaponless mother, wielding his power even once I'd been shackled. "Oh my God," I repeat, trying to see through the blinding rays from his high beam light. I look at the cop as best I can, shaking my head, thinking of the neighbor's sangria I'd turned down and the dinner I'd just eaten. In the video you see me seated on the ground, a spotlight cast in a perfect circle around me. You hear me replying with the truth as if reading from a bad TV script of a strangely theatrical scene:

Dramatically lit by the lighting designer, attention drawn to the grey-haired woman sitting cross-legged on the corner of her lot, her arms for some reason pulled behind her, she is surrounded by police and police cars. The light from the cop's flashlight is intense on her, hollowing her eyes, which seem to be searching as she stares into the beam. Around that white circle all is dark, and beyond that dark all is light again, striped and chaotic from the twirling lights atop the cop cars. How did she get here? Was she not, just moments ago, involved in the problem of making the perfect hot cocoa? As they pick her up and lead her to the squad car, she is shouting orders over the fence to her husband who has started to run into the house to get her wallet after the police ask for her ID. He freezes when the cops shout, "She won't need ID in the cell anyway don't bother." The husband has been running through the yard finally with a job he can act upon, freezes as it is cancelled, begins to run back to the scene with his wife, perhaps to be present, perhaps to witness, perhaps to bless her goodbye as this ridiculousness becomes even more frightening, but she is almost in the car now and can only shout the distance across the fence, shouting what is paramount on her mind this moment, which of course, (as for all criminals who roll out of their houses to assault police) is the hot cocoa, still on the stove, still in the big pot she'd transferred it to when the smaller pot looked like it might overflow. For all she knows that cocoa is going to boil over, make a mess, and form the skin no one likes, maybe even separating the milk irreversibly. She is shouting to her husband who runs across the yard in the direction of the kitchen per her instructions, to do this something for her, to do her bidding, to make things right—for her, for the safety of the kitchen, for the party. As her head ducks into the squad car (how awkward to have hands locked behind you and try to enter a car and sit down—she'd never noticed that), she is shouting to him desperately, so that even now writing this, the computer screen is blurred by her tears, her sobbing, the memory of trying to salvage the hot cocoa, of projecting with all her strength and surely carrying words over the fence into her husband's heart: "The hot cocoa, it's still on, it's on the stove, the stove is on, you must turn it off, it may be boiling, it could boil over—did you hear me, could you hear me?"

Scene change: *We momentarily see her quite humorless, in shock in the cell, remembering the above scene. She appears to be ill. She shakes her head side to side and mutters to herself as if recalling a sour taste. "Really?" she whispers in disbelief. And then, with the faintest remnant of humor....*

Flash back: *She is sitting cross-legged under the bully cop's beam; close up of cop's expression of disdain as he speaks his line:*

BULLY COP:
I bet you've been drinking.

The scene is cast like a bizarre Ionesco play with the spotlight encircling her perfectly so that out of context it seems she is meditating, her arms locked in an ancient mudra behind her, her legs in sukhasana, "easy pose," her face looking up to the angry man who has used his power, such that, to write the scene, the script-writer gags and feels vomit surface, and to whom the seated woman with resignation now says, shaking her head in disbelief because she knows this isn't a comedy, although neither can it be a real play, for no one would believe it—

SEATED WOMAN:
No, Sir. I have not been drinking. I just had tofu.
With broccoli.

"ALVAREZ!" Alexa's name was shouted with the crazy clang of the metal door, and she was on her feet as if by pogo stick, awake and alert. She was led out for a while, probably for thumb printing, and when she returned to the cell, we talked.

Alexa was arrested because her ex claimed she'd assaulted him. Recall it was Hallowe'en, a holiday Alexa said at least eight times was her favorite of all holidays. Her ex had agreed she could pick up the kids at 1:00 p.m. after her work shift. Hallowe'en was "her holiday," her rotation to have the kids. Alexa and her two boys would go to Michael's Art Supply store to get decorations, some face make-up, and details for their costumes, then to her apartment to prepare.

But when she got to the ex's he said the kids weren't ready and blocked her from the door. He insisted she come back at 3:00 p.m. This she did, although her home was too far away for her to go there and back. She killed two hours grocery shopping. Emotionally, she tried to see the time mix-up as a misunderstanding.

At 3:00 p.m., when she returned, the ex said the kids were now at his mom's, another distance away. Their belongings were just upstairs, he said, and if she wanted their weekend bags she could go up and get them. Alexa didn't want to enter and didn't want to go up the stairs. Arguing ensued.

The details are fuzzy, but this I remember. When Alexa tried to leave, her ex blocked the car door. He began to kick her car window repeatedly. She tried to make a call, he grabbed her cell phone and smashed it. Alexa punched his shoulder. It was this assault claim her ex-husband later filed. Police came to her door that night after trick-or-treating was over, the two young boys asleep, Alexa in a Princeton sweatshirt and her boyfriend's boxers. She was shown a warrant, was handcuffed, and we soon met each other in a cell.

We went back and forth about Alexa's options for a long, focused span of cell time, that stunning clock that has no face and never ticks. A month later, I would be swimming in a pool to try to cool my nervous system still racing, my inflamed ears and red face, and when I saw the pool wall was empty, missing its clock, I felt it again. That feeling of privilege, of having the privilege to expect a clock to be there, to tell the management *There is no clock.*

Privilege would follow me everywhere after that one night in jail—when I'd want a sip of water and just go pour some, when I'd reach for ChapStick right there in my purse which was right there on my shoulder, when I'd decide to throw on one more blanket at night against the cold until, like Goldilocks, I was just right. So many tiny privileges every tiny moment of my tiny life. Time was just one of them.

When a new woman would be slammed into the cell, one of our first questions would be *Did you notice the time?* For in the absence of a watch, a cell phone, a clock, time is both halted and edgy. At any point, the vast unknown span of hours could be interrupted by the clang of keys and the bang of heavy locks followed by the shout of a cellmate's name. The word "holding cell" is only too accurate. Time was held, bladders were held, anger was held, sleep was held, information was withheld, and all power was gone. I didn't organize everyone into a yoga practice because not only could I not breathe, not only did my stomach feel like a drill was stuck in it, spinning, not only was I shaking too violently to consider a yoga *asana* let alone to take successful fingerprints, but not knowing the *when* of anything meant one could do nothing pro-active with one's time. They'd found a way to reduce us beyond cold, scared, thirsty, and hungry, to unhinge us from time and place. For it was 1:00 a.m. or 2:00 a.m. or 4:00 a.m., or some hammocked span of non-moving time owned by someone else and we had no information as to how much time it would be. I spent my time talking with cellmates in an exchange of our stories—or "cases" rather, for I was soon to realize I'd become "a case"—careful to read faces and make overtures if the face was available and safe. Alexa, in her French-braided, toilet-papered hair, her fitted prison jumpsuit, and her blue booties, read safe to me, and I had every reason to believe her version of the truth. Why stand in the cold timelessness wondering if your cellmates were crazy when you could find out who they were and help each other not become crazy now? This intimacy could be interrupted at any second of course, but at least we had voice and face to rock against, and the sounds of our words and our stories made us human.

INTERMEZZO 2

Bullies:
America's Pride and Shame

———

I AM IN THE GRANVILLE Island Market in Vancouver and a woman at a stall asks me if I'd like to try her organic skincare products. I tell her that's exactly what I'd like to do, and in time, as she demonstrates professional and notably loving hands making circular motions around her eyes with a carrot seed facial crème, I reveal to her that it was a reactionary response to an assault, which originally triggered my skin inflammation and ill health.

I don't tell her the assaulters were police.

I'm in Canada for God's sake.

I am thinking about this in a train of thought regarding Donald Trump and the shame we Americans carry abroad. Shame to reveal that police kicked me down in my backyard and incarcerated me. Shame that we'd promote someone who acts like a bully, sells himself proudly as a bully, and encourages bullying— in rallies, in policies, throughout his campaign style, and in lashing tweets as president.

Bullies have Energy. They create movement like a fast river running on its own momentum, undeterred by Stuff in the way. The motion of a bully is almost beautiful in its unstoppable current— the pure rush of it, the swell, the force. It takes with it any pliable piece—rock or branch or swimmer—and leaves behind only what is too rooted to move. In the still, quiet, stream afterwards, exactly what just whooshed past, and how its momentum built so powerfully, is contemplated only by those stuck to shore.

Most of us first come across bullying in school, whether as victims or perpetrators or as both. But it is much more significant in human affairs than a bit of pushing and name calling in the playground. Rooted in the abuse of power, bullying is to be found wherever there are differences in power between people...

—From *Bullying and the Abuse of Power Project,*

INTERDISCIPLINARY.NET

The disrespect from the law officers astounded me. But the beauty of a bully is the lack of pretense and the absence of any other point of view. My point of view was that I was a Mom who at that moment was making hot cocoa for twenty-five kids in my backyard.

Their point of view was they were on a case, I didn't belong in the scene they'd constructed, and I needed to be removed.

Anyone can be bullied, and anyone can bully. And so bullying is to be found in sport... in prisons, police stations and army camps; in education at all levels, from kindergarten to university, among both staff and students; in workplaces of all kinds – in offices and factories, hospitals and shops; in the media, and in the corridors of power.

But I am a stayed branch, not the movable one they envisioned. I have planted and replanted myself to be an active, rooted participant in my home life. I have trained myself to be in this town in this house available to my children for their upbringing and my clients for my work. Have I wanted to follow fast-moving waters and go elsewhere? A hundred times yes—after 911, The Sniper, Anthrax, to name a few. I have stayed to see my work through.

I live here, I explained.
It meant nothing.

I am the mother.
It meant nothing.

I am the adult parent responsible for these minors. This is my home, I explained again.

The notion that they couldn't hear me was intensifying. Surely if I selected the right words they would understand.

But this is not the mindset of bully. Bully plows forward and with him or her comes a sweep of available bodies. Either these are destroyed or they join the froth, adding weight and wave to the river.

Bullying is present in every sphere of life, in every country...
It leads to human beings and human life being diminished
rather than enhanced. It can ruin lives, and it can end lives.

I directed my words to the two women cops, one white, one Black, blocking my way out of my gate. *I've known these kids since Kindergarten,* I said, but I was editing the boys' detail that mattered to me—my son's passionate lisp when he announced one day as if His Lordship had arrived to Kindergarten: *there's a new boy in our class and his name is Dzulian.* I was editing how he'd pronounced Julian's name with Zsa Zsa Gabor's accent and

Louie Armstrong's growl. I wanted to say that Julian's mom is my close friend, that we love to walk around the park together, as if that too would substantiate us, provide ID for the "who" of who we are.

Months later I met women whose sons had been killed by police, who sat before audiences on panels and started their stories with, "My son was a straight-A student," or "He was a supervisor at his job and in his second year of college," or "He was engaged to be married," as if to communicate to our unhearing ears, as if to get through that blocked gate, as if to e*xplain*, for god's sake, that these are—were—their *valuable* sons.

"Be kind whenever possible. It is always possible," are the words posted above my cutting board. I try to live up to that quote by the Dalai Lama. And I was trained in stress reduction for law enforcement. So I was sure that with the right choice of words and good intention I could connect with these police officers— woman to woman, human to human.

There were two sets of losers in the bully scenario my skin still recalls.

First, there was me, my family, and the high schoolers whose first Facebook post after these events said, "Mikey's mom got beat up by the cops." These are the teens who will soon move into adulthood. They have filed in their minds that the police don't listen and are not their friends.

Second, there was the team of officers whose actions we reported to the Internal Affairs Office, and who are now, one would assume, angry for that too—this pain in the neck older woman who got them in trouble. Seven police officers—male and female, Black and white—burst into her yard and pulled out teens they wrongly suspected had assaulted someone. The parents were within eyesight and earshot and easily could have been consulted. The youth named Julian, forcibly pushed by a policeman into the alley, had asked incredulously, "Aren't you going to speak to the property owners—the parents in charge?"

But self-reflection would slow a bully just like a dam slows a river. They could not, or did not, pause to think. My presence in the scene was simply in the way of their *momentum*, so they took me down.

"Now we've got another problem," the skinny cop guarding my son said with scorn, looking down at me seated on the ground in handcuffs. This, I later heard on video.

"Yeah," said my son. "My mom. She's a real problem."

It manifests itself in many ways—from simple name calling to perverse psychological cruelty; from insults aimed at individuals, to grave injustices perpetrated against groups of people, on account of religious beliefs, lifestyle, race or national identity. It includes religious and sexual intolerance; the abuse of political, personal, and economic power; and both physical and sexual violence.

How was "recovery" possible when—nationwide—the reports of police brutality were relentless? Colleagues used the word "healing" as if what happened would resolve, with breathing techniques and time. But I wanted to shout from the rooftops, I wanted to organize a march with placards that read: IF YOU MESS WITH MAMA BEAR EXPECT A RESPONSE and, DE-ESCALATION TRAINING NOW! I wanted TV to know, and newspapers, and neighbors, and senators. This was not about "feeling better." I no longer wanted to live in my home. My county. My country. This planet. Because if this could happen to *me*…

If I could be a victim in this drama, what if instead of three teens (two white, one Black), only one teen had ended up with these police? What if that teen had been stopped at the park instead of our house? What if, when they'd walked to get an electrical cord for the sound system from another teen's car, one of the kids had gone alone? What if the car owner (a slender, Filipino teen in pink Polo shirt) had gone alone to his car as he'd originally suggested? Or the slightly taller (African American) teen—in hooded Hallowe'en gear—had gone alone, after insisting "No, I better go," feeling protective of his smaller friend in case there were rough kids at the park (which there were). What if instead of my son and Julian (both white but in Ninja costume) accompanying their Black friend to protect *him*, that friend had been confronted solo in the dark park by seven riled-up cops on a search, and what if he could only offer this weak explanation, "No, I don't live in this neighborhood. I was getting a part from my friend's car." *And where were you headed?* "Umm...to a party down that alley."

Oh God, what if?

The Canadian skincare saleswoman and I lock eyes. This pulls me to the present, to the market, and my flashback sinks into its secret cove. I'm glad my son finished his college application that fated Hallowe'en night, and was accepted to UBC, the University of British Columbia in Vancouver, with tuition half the price of American options, plus a scholarship. Canada seems gentler, and this saleswoman really listens; I could easily dissolve into the warmth of her eyes, well-lotioned with soothing carrot-seed balm.

I buy two products, but like every product I've tried, neither the carrot seed nor the hemp balm will resolve the skin welts along my face, my ears, my neck and scalp. "Healing," I figure, will have to come from some anti-inflammatory to my heart and soul.

And no, I never did tell her that my assaulters were police, law enforcement officers of Montgomery County, Maryland. She was such a kind woman. I didn't wish to shame my America further.

CHAPTER 3

Richmond

———

sur·ren·der | \ sə-ˈren-dər \
surrendered; surrendering\ sə-ˈren-d(ə-)riŋ \

transitive verb

to yield to the power, control, or possession of another
upon compulsion or demand

—Merriam-Webster

RICHMOND

RICHMOND GOT IT. RICHMOND, MY *cellmate—I never learned her name, but she was from Richmond, California and I too had been raised in the Bay Area—got the notion of surrender, but for her it became her life. She was perhaps twenty. She first surrendered when she was sixteen. Some asshole boyfriend threatened her to work as his whore—her words—and she kept at it. She told me she just doesn't know any other work now.*

"It's hard to change," she said. "It's the only way I know to make a living."

I wanted to argue with her, but my adult and teenage boys have raised me well. I just listened.

"Yeah, patterns are really hard to break," I said after a while. "I mean, you have to trick patterns, outwit them, or they just win."

She looked at me. Richmond is Asian American. Black hair past her shoulders. Blue-black sheen to her thick hair like Veronica Lodge in the Archie Comics. Thick-framed glasses that made her look studious-smart. Eyebrows that arched like an actor angling a brow to ask a question. Fine features and perfect skin on a strong, pretty, linebacker's body. She was wearing a long-sleeved shirt over leggings, a layer of soft belly bulging over the waist band. Lucky Richmond, the warmest of us all, for the cop who pulled her in had suggested she change out of her "work clothes" and into something more appropriate for an arrest. The cop herself had plucked clothes from Richmond's suitcase saying, "It's cold in jail—here, why don't you put these on," choosing a pullover sweater and something like a flannel shirt my dad would wear in Vermont. I remember thinking that was decent copping, choosing cozy, presentable clothes for your handcuffed party.

Our eye contact was staggering. Like Baby, Richmond held back nothing with her eyes. For a moment, had someone watched us, they might have thought we were having a staring contest, standing up, facing off. Until I started mumbling that is, half-talking to myself.

"The only way I know to overpower a pattern is to put something next to it that you love more. Something about life that you love more; something in life that you want more than what you have."

I didn't want to lecture her. But I was there for a reason, that I knew. And if the reason was to plant a seed in Richmond, who'd been pulled in for prostitution when two men were questioned following sessions with her—she the one now in jail, the snitchers free to walk—well, then I was going to use our jail time well and spout some words. It's interesting how being older with grey hair can make you seem safe. Or wise or something. Or accessible.

WHEN I WATCH THE VIDEO clip, it is as if I watch a silent nightmare I had that now has audio put to it, something ears can hear and eyes can see as if it happened, really happened, somewhere far away from this writing table where I sit, though were I to open the orange Venetian blind, I could see the back gate, the alley and the side street where the cop car drove me away in handcuffs.

Big deal, part of me says. A little drama. *What doesn't kill you makes you strong.*

I'm drawn to make sense, to rationalize as if, *Hey, everyone gets a little police beat up in their life, right?*

How wacky, the way we become used to abuse and begin to shrug our shoulders as if it's the new normal and anyone who can't adjust has a problem. I return to my husband and son over and over to fight for speaking rights. Their patterning is head down, mouth closed, privacy-privacy. I'm refusing it. I'm saying, *shout this one from the haystack. Shout this one from the top of the hills. Shout this one to the nation.* Where do we get the idea of shame, and how is it torqued to feel that way? It's yet another twisting to make sure we don't speak, we stay powerless.

I hear my videoed voice when the cops are holding me down, the distorted sound of my shout YOU'RE HURTING ME, that comes out like some gremlin rebirthed into the Wicked Witch of the West when she is melting to the sand. My face is down in Autumn's sweet first leaves, and my face is in dirt and grass. My face is on the land we hemmed and hawed over before finally cutting down the old privet, giving up on it after we tried endless trimming and weeding, and planting more privet didn't close the gaps. Instead, finally, we chose a tall wood fence, and it is beside that fence that my cheek now lies, turned to the left where my son managed to capture on video, a little bit of face in the dark.

"Stop resisting or I'm going to have to tase you!" the cop wrenching my right arm says. And then the sound of my son, dear one, the sound of my younger son's voice—registering in me like some intravenous drug to my bloodstream—

"Mom—Mom! You've got to do it—MOM!"

And you wonder at the strength of a teenaged youth, to stand surrounded by cops and videotape his mom taken down by more cops, speaking out on her behalf—"She's a sixty-year-old woman—she's not going to hurt anyone!" Managing to shout to me, reason with cops, and keep the video going the same time—against the expressed wishes of the tall cop to his right—how did he keep his wits?

And then this…it comes around again to this: How did the men stand there. How did my men stand there and watch this. How did they stand there and use reason and restraint. My son was surrounded by cops only a few feet from where I was taken down: he counseled me and potentially saved my life; he videotaped—even when told not to; he documented the truth.

"I have a right to do this," he said, age seventeen, to the cop on his right, and kept videotaping his mom in the dirt with two cops on her back. How did he swallow his fear and do that? And how did it break him to watch. "You have a right to do a lot of things," the cop sarcastically replied.

My husband is 6'3" and 230 lbs. Every one of the seven cops was shorter and smaller than him. He knew better than to add fire to the mix—someone could get shot. He stayed still. He didn't shout. He did what was right.

But how did my husband not move, not move, not move, not jump in on my behalf. What part of his heart imploded to stand still through those violent minutes? How did he use his knowing of guns and batons and tasers and handcuffs and police cars and numbers and power and the law on the side of the police, to keep himself still and restrained?

How smart of him.

How very very smart.

And how much worse the outcome could have been. How dangerous. How final. How catastrophic it could have been.

Seven police with tasers and guns, four of whom will later sign to a story told their way, threatening my life further with thirteen years in jail. For they will say that I assaulted them.

How smart my men were. How knowledgeable. How street wise. How clear-thinking.

Pause.

All hell broke loose right here, two years after writing this chapter. I was trying to edit it, and I walked away confused. Gave myself a little time to think. Because that one segment where I paused had been through many edits up and down. That section had been expressed and then suppressed.

Because it was about my husband. Because it was about him not being there, not outraged, not defending me. Because it was about my surrender in front of him, absent of his activation. I am an easily activated person—witness that I was activated by the alerting teen girl who came convulsing into my kitchen, and once I heard that kids had been removed by the police I was out there.

Did I overreact or did I meet up to bully energy and refute it in favor of standing by my kids? Regardless, I was surely activated.

I love the grounded-ness of my husband. I feel a safety with him in that regard. My bowels relax beside him; the world is a safer place. But at that moment his grounded-ness perhaps overwhelmed his activation source. He did nothing in terms of immediate response. That is hard to reflect on. And it harbored as tension between us. I wrote about it in this chapter. Then months later, upon reading it and thinking about others reading it—strangers who I might not trust, friends who I don't wish to prejudice or in front of whom I don't wish to question my husband—I edited that section out.

I edited it out, and then two years later, here in the Salt Spring Island library, British Columbia, Canada, I looked at it again. Thought to myself, who do I owe the full story to? Who do I owe protection and privacy to? How far am I willing to be with honesty? What if "honesty" informs and frees some readers, but hurts another?

I remember certain phrases of my first mother's. I was four or five when she said:

"Sometimes it's okay to tell a lie. To not tell the whole truth. If it does less harm to someone, then it's okay."

But she was hinting at a very dark something. She was dying. She knew it. I asked her about it because I also, at such a young age, knew it.

"Are you dying, Mommy?"

"I'm trying not to," she replied.

That was not the worst of her half-lies; there were other more blatant moments of not telling the whole truth. It was the style then with death, and my young parents, hit with cancer before cancer was common, did their best. Her desire was to spare me, and to spare my sisters. There was no sparing, though. Perhaps she might have known.

Is there no sparing the truth of what happened on October 31, 2014, and how that impacted me, my family, my marriage? There is no sparing of that truth. That harsh truth is what we Americans face with a cycle of violence among citizens and among law enforcement, a cycle of violence that may reach its peak with a president willing to spew hate language ad hoc as he walked the campaign trail and as he governs. Can we look ourselves in the eye as a country and say what is real? In the context of my personal hit from this violence can I look it in the eye and say what is real? Can I write it, can you read it, and know also the super-human effort it's taken husband and wife to stay in the fire of this pain and work to emerge stronger afterwards?

We nearly did not make it. I put Chapter Three on hold for that day some four weeks ago, when I thought it needed just overnight to rest. I thought, hmmm, maybe husband would be willing to write his own segment for this chapter, saying what it was like for him to witness this assault and why he never wanted to speak of it thereafter.

The night I paused to let the chapter gestate we had a plan to go to a movie. We also had a plan to meet and discuss a personal issue between us. We were to do that at 6:00 p.m. before the movie; or if that couldn't happen, at 9:00 p.m. after the movie. We're not usually so planned out, but this was important.

Husband was in charge of remembering the time and plan for our meeting. Why? Because he'd been tired the night before and needed to end a valuable conversation. Promised he'd pick it up again. I asked for a time, he set the time. I asked him to be in charge. I told him in a friendly but sincere voice that I wouldn't remind him. He likes reminders in writing: "I'll write it on my hand," he'd said. "I'll put it in my phone."

Six p.m. came and went. Movie time. It was *Wonder Woman*. I'm a handful to be with in an action movie and most people shouldn't go with me. My husband held me through much of my thigh-grabbing and arm pinching, and we were glad we went. But were we colored by the movie—was husband influenced by Wonder Woman and her lover moving at terrific speed to do good in the world? Was I influenced by her power and independence?

Nine p.m. came and went. Nine-thirty. Husband didn't orient us toward our meeting time. We were in a car on a winding road, headed back up the mountain to a friend's cottage we'd rented for the month while here to write our books. I wondered how to broach the topic. I'd promised I wouldn't remind him. How would I remind him without reminding him?

I finally said as he drove: "There's something I'm not supposed to remind you about."

"What?" he asked while winding a particular hairpin near Bishops Walk.

"If I told you, I'd be reminding you, and I promised I wouldn't remind you."

"That's a power play, don't do that," he said.

"No-nnnnn-no, I'm not doing a power play. You said you'd be in charge of remembering something, remember?"

"That is exactly a power play—you're withholding information," he said, and then said more that I can't retell, using language I have never heard from him, and a rising anger I've never seen up close in unsafe quarters. Nothing about this was typical.

He began to rage and drive at high speed. Perhaps he was Wonder Woman's lover on his motorbike, perhaps he was Wonder Woman going it alone after the Nazis.

I can't tell you the speed. It was in kilometers and I was too dizzy to read the meter. We were going dangerously fast; I was hanging on to the passenger's handle contemplating how to get out of the car. It was night. I did not wish to be alone walking on this shoulder-less road. What was my safest outcome—to wait it out? To jump out? To insist on being let out and then hitchhike at night? Or go knock on a stranger's door? Who would I tell without drawing the law to implicate my husband? I sat it out, gripping the door handle; I watched the road with utter vigilance.

I screamed when I saw the fawn.

Golden. Eyes huge.

Smack center of the road. Like someone set her there, the tiniest, skinniest one ever. Smack center.

Spotlighted by our headlights. I screamed. He screeched the brakes. We came near, we didn't hit.

Golden fawn just stood there and took it. Her eyes growing huge as bowls in our headlights. Deep bowls, insisting and insisting: *You will stop. You will be sane. You will stop this. You will face yourself through me.*

I have to stop this writing now. I have someone to meet; the woman whose cottage we were headed to, who still knows nothing about what this "healing island" wrought upon our marriage. She will later tell me that by "healing," she'd meant going through the fire. She will later say marriages often break up when people come to this island. She will also tell me there are too many suicides here. Troubled youth gravitate to this island seeking refuge, and too often take their own lives. I believed her of course, but it wasn't until I witnessed it myself that the burden on this island really penetrated and I got it that this wasn't about crystal vortexes, but life and death and the critical timing of getting help for traumatized youth. I was xeroxing a chapter of my book in a print shop when a man began to scream.

The print shop door was wide open to let the cool summer air in when a young man literally threw himself on the wooden promenade—just on the other side of the glass window where I was xeroxing. If I'd reached my arm through the window, I'd have touched him. Was he having a seizure? A bad trip? His guttural screams were horrific and non-stop; his body thrashed on the boardwalk like demons were on him. Two other young men ran up the stairs to the boardwalk, one to wrestle the man into his arms and hold him weeping and writhing, the other to pop his head into the print shop door to explain this: *The man's best friend was just found hung beneath the bridge to the peace garden.*

I had paused the book right here at this point. To think and consider how to speak the truth or how to shape it to be palatable. How to protect my beloved. How to protect the reader. But it was as if the fawn was there to help us avoid another island tragedy, saying *No. I am the stark truth just short of being exploded. Follow that rage, follow that activation. FOLLOW THAT ACTIVATION.* For my husband's rage spoke truth. It spoke of his power and how it was quelled when it should have been loud. Now it was loud when it could have been spoken and heard.

We are both in shock from what has exploded between us. I am up all night in the cottage, studying the bios of every couples counselor in the vicinity. The dissolution of our marriage is in front of us. We are facing it with a sadness bordering on collective despair and at times for me, suicidal despair. We have been together for thirty-nine years and the end is smack in our face. For the first time I know I cannot weep this one out alone; I cannot write and dance it out of my body, our lives. I can't clear my chakras enough to rectify the magnitude of his harbored rage revealed. It was real and to be honored as such: there was no lie to it. It was anger I'd wanted to see two years before, directed at police brutality. Now we needed help and I could not be the therapist.

Then we hear about Charlottesville. And I read a word spoken over and over, the word "outrage." The righteousness of good healthy outrage when outrage is the response that meets the energy of violence and says *no* to hate. *No to hate.* In my backyard; in my family; in your family; in our city; in your city; in our country. Yes to healthy outrage. Yes to listening and looking at the source of the violence and the story behind it. Yes to weeping and sitting with oneself first before one acts. But yes to outrage.

We find a couples counselor. We enter the heat of another fire: being real, being open—on a level that is like the local oysters opening their strong shell only so far, that gelatinous animal body having no skin. Then we open farther. We salvage our marriage knowing there's no going back. We are like the families who've seen their homes explode in war—can we salvage our lives? The shell is open, our raw bodies have been torched. We cannot *not* be different now.

Four weeks after this personal explosion, I feel solid enough to rewrite this part of the chapter. To continue forward, upward, with the marriage now truer than ever. To continue with my story.

For you see, I was there. There I really was. I was there in the alley with the cops on my back. I was there, walking with them twisting my arms behind me, not fathoming what they were trying to do, let alone consciously trying to defy them. They were wrenching my arms, I tried to wrench them away. They were twisting them behind me, I tried to twist them out of their grasp. The notion that they were trying to handcuff didn't occur to me. Why on earth would they be handcuffing me?

The phrase, "That's resisting arrest!" didn't even compute. How would it be resisting arrest when no one had declared anyone under arrest. And it surely wasn't me because *I was just walking to my son!* As I'd told the first cops I would do.

Perhaps I took in Mikey's voice, perhaps it was his instructive, pleading voice when the cop threatened to tase me—*Mom, you've got to do it*—that counseled me to let their touch do what their touch demanded to do. There is knowledge within the body of surrender.

There is knowledge of what *surrender* refers to. It refers to giving up or dying. It refers to letting the power overpower you for the sake of living another moment. It refers to less harm than the extreme harm even if either harm is wrong.

It is surrender. Do you know what that means? That overpowering is a rape of the heart. It is the violation of the sacred. It is the murder of the spirit. That moment is an experience of surrendering *right*, giving it over, giving it up as if it was always wrong. There is no more right then. There is only surrender to some semblance of safety, though the "safety" means being handcuffed, means a cop car, means a jail cell, means a toilet under videotape that is projected in the jail hall. Means hate coming from more sides than you ever imagined. It means surrendering to a darkness so dark it has no taste, but you will get to know it over and over again soon enough. For it will replay in your muscle memory, your nightmares, your endocrine output. And all this to live? To live with limbs intact? To live without tasing damage or resulting death? To survive my own backyard for god's sake, to survive my own kid's party? To survive my neighborhood police now assaulting me at my home?

Surrender is a thing women finally learn to do. They learn it when a man overpowers them in a sex crime. They learn it as sex workers. They learn it in war. They learn it in domestic violence, when they know there's no escape, or they know to stand in front of their kids, surrendering their own body as guard. Women, who fight and rage and shout, surrender when they know that last moment is a choice of skin or no skin, safe children or no children. And if the assault doesn't kill them, the surrender might just.

For surrender is a piece of your heart taken. It is a mold that then grows rampant. It is a chemistry redistributed through your bloodstream with zeal and potency. It is a weed in your relationships. And then there is nothing to be done but what I am doing. Weep till the cows come home. Shout for the right to speak. Write the words even if they sting like acid vomit as you type. Streak your face with tears and your scalp with rashes. Heat your vessel with passion and hurt and anger and desperation. And seek light. Seek light. Seek light in crevices between fat ugly boulders, but for fuck's sake, seek it.

I think of you a lot, Richmond. I think of the strength it will take for you to consider rebuilding yourself with a different identity. The strength it will take for you to undo your surrender and fight life all over again.

For you've surrendered to the pattern now. It's the norm for you. You know it; it works; you have a relationship to the world through this life. To break it is to stand up to life all over again. It might as well be standing up to a tsunami. Seems like the wave upon wave will break on your head and over you and take you down—one way or another take you down. You imagine it's best to *stop resisting* and roll with it, landing with your porcelain-smooth cheek turned left, a little bit of face in the dark.

But now some woman three times your age, sharing a cell with you for one night of lost revenue, has suggested you stand up like a fool and brace up against that wave. You are interested. I can hear the craving. I worry for you Richmond, that the unknowns will knock your tender hopes down if you try. I worry that you don't have a chance; that you might have been the smart one to surrender body first.

INTERMEZZO 3

Silent Vigil

———

IT WAS WIN-WIN. I'D serve my Community Service hours at my local homeless shelter; I'd offer an extra set of hands, in the kitchen serving meals or chopping vegetables, or in the store sorting clothes. My case worker had given me permission to ask the management if I could work there, so convenient to my house: Progress Place, where I'd donated clothing for years, dropping off bag-loads of useful stuff, with the kids in the back seat of the car, or simply walking over there— I like carrying heavy loads.

I walked the eight blocks or so down Bonifant, up Grove, through the alley to Fenton, past a selection of Ethiopian cafes, restaurants, crepe shops, along Silver Spring Avenue, past Sky House Yoga Studio and Kaldi's Coffee Shop, across Georgia Avenue near the railroad tracks, to the impressive glass doors of Progress Place.

I explained to the woman at the reception counter that I wanted to speak to management about serving my Community Hours there. She told me the right contact person's name, but that he wasn't in. "Try 4:00 p.m. tomorrow," she said.

At 3:45 the next day I set out again. I was feeling relatively positive. The lawyer had not only negotiated in private with the prosecuting attorney to drop all criminal charges against me, of which there were four: assault of police officers, interfering with an investigation, creating a public disturbance, and resisting arrest; but he'd also argued down a last-minute slap of thirty-six community service hours—the prosecutor's attempt to save face for the police. The lawyer had proudly reported his success in reducing my hours to twenty-four by cleverly starting with a low comeback of fifteen.

I had been surprised by *any* hours, however, and showed little elation. I was still chilled by the court appearance and then the mandatory signing of a contract in which I had to swear I would not sue the Montgomery County Police, in exchange for which my case would be cleared from record. Then there was this little P.S. of Community Service Hours. Lest I thought I'd "won" in any way, these hours communicated clearly who still held power and who still needed to be punished: law enforcement was posturing as magnanimous to let me off so easy—this time—but let's not forget I had committed a crime. I must pay back society for my errors.

Underneath the prosecutor's expungement of my record was of course fear—that trying to lock me in jail for any portion of the thirteen-years maximum sentence could backfire against them. But at the same time, they had to maintain that I'd been a victim of police brutality for good reason. If they didn't play their cards right, I might go public, nail them, go to the press or TV. They didn't know I was the last Neanderthal and knew zilch about social media. Regardless, I might throw in the towel and sue them for damages. I had that video after all: thirty seconds that showed exactly who'd assaulted whom.

But why *didn't* I sue them? Several reasons—foremost was the lawyer's expert opinion that the Fraternal Order of Police is all-powerful and I could lose the case. Second, my husband and I didn't want to spend the next year or two of our lives in and out of court, replaying this unpleasant experience while fighting for justice. Third, it was our last child's senior year of high school and spending it in drama and conflict would have been our loss. Fourth, we didn't have the money to pay a lawyer for ongoing services in a case we could really lose. Fifth, there was enough suffering to recover from.

It was now mid-December and a week had passed since my court date, during which I'd ignored the mandate to perform these community service hours and now I didn't want to miss the deadline to fulfill them. Christmas was coming; I could get caught in the holiday closings. Renee the caseworker had suggested Habitat for Humanity's warehouse and store, but it was north a way, up Route 29, and finding new places was a hurdle for me these days. I had to travel in daytime only, and either on foot or along a driving path I knew.

Every step in the world was scary—even the mirror while brushing my teeth could morph into a scene from the police assault, and unpredictably I could be thrust into what I came to know as a "daymare," where day, almost as dangerous as night, could transform a safe, innocuous moment, an everyday activity, a word on a page, a sharp pencil, a pain in my shoulder, a blasting image shooting through my mind—everything involuntarily could attack me, such was the unsafe world. Getting gas at a gas station was way too vulnerable; shopping in the aisles of a brightly lit store I had a three-minute threshold like a soft egg; going to a "floor barre" class—so wonderful for a dancer's alignment— seemed fine, of course, until the teacher did a neck warm-up with our hands clasped behind our backs: I sank to the floor with a weakness overriding my strong legs and tears that continued through the 75-minute class, so unexpected was the trigger of handcuffs. Even seeing caring neighbors was a reminder of the crazy experience I held in my head, images that weren't normal, with police, jail guards, cellmates I'd met who no one else had met. On what level could I communicate? My sweet neighborhood now felt poisonous to me and not to them. For a year I avoided my backyard.

But Progress Place was a community of hope; I felt purposeful about doing my community service there. And the men I stepped around as they sat on the front steps were friendly enough, harmless even if inebriated, sprawled over the porch stairs in hats and parkas against the December threat of rain.

The manager I was to speak to was here this time, the receptionist told me. "Walk through the kitchen to the far end, you'll see his office," she said.

It was before the dinner rush, and two kitchen staff stood relaxed near the big basin sinks as I entered. I paused to greet them. "Hello, I'm headed to speak with the manager," I said, before walking through their turf. A large, aproned man with hands like mitts shook my gloved hand and welcomed me. The small man beside him nodded a greeting. *How warm*, I thought. *This was so the right place to choose.* I'd worked in many restaurants and pictured us working together for my service hours and maybe beyond, as it seemed we'd enjoy one another's camaraderie and efficiency in this kitchen.

The manager was in his office; he looked up with a strained face. *Perhaps he has a lot of concerns*, I thought. I smiled at him with the spirit of the kitchen folk I'd just passed. His fit frame was buttoned up in a green shirt and grey pants, belted at a slender waist—no extra fat on this man. His hair was tight to his head, like President Obama's, but less of it. I explained why I was looking for him and presented my Community Service Hours card.

"Why were you arrested?" he asked, standing.

"It was a confluence of errors that occurred," I said. "My case was expunged." I had recently learned that word, as one learns the vocabulary of the law pertaining to one's own case. Who knew this word before? Many of my well-educated friends drew a blank when I used that word later; but of course this man would know the language.

"If it was assault, you can't work here," he replied.

Perhaps he was—well, not joking exactly, but reciting something he had to recite?

"Well, it was Assault of a Police Officer, but clearly they were found to be in error: the case has been expunged."

"If it was assault, you can't work here," he repeated. There was a smile missing. I tried smiling.

I was again trying to communicate with someone whose face was set, frozen, absent of human expression. Clearly, he didn't understand. Clearly, I still believed I had capacities to reach unreachable humans and kept trying.

"I can bring my expungement papers for you to see. My case has been expunged."

Pause.

"Totally expunged," I said, as if adding the redundant word "totally" to an already thorough word—defined as "erase or remove completely (something unwanted or unpleasant)" by Webster's—would help him understand the absolution of a criminal record. Expungement implied, of course, innocence, but in case that wasn't obvious, I explained that too.

"They assaulted me, but rewrote the truth to cover themselves," I said. Was I digging myself into a hole? Surely not, surely this brown-skinned man in management of a homeless shelter knew how the system worked, and just needed to see the appropriate papers confirming the truth of my story: "I live nearby, I'll just get you my papers."

"It doesn't matter," he said. "Once you've assaulted someone, you can't work here."

"But I didn't assault anyone!" I said. "Even the court confirmed that."

"It doesn't matter," he said.

He started to back away from me, but the only space he had to go was the tiniest of offices, no windows, a closet really. I felt aggressive before him, taller than he was, my frame in the doorway as he backed up. Surely, I now enacted the assaulter who was a danger to have in this homeless shelter.

He looked scared—might he call the police on me? His distrust colored me in, as if my body's outline said *criminal* in his door frame, and, coloring me *in* activated my volatility like Frankenstein's monster coming to life. *Fee, fie, foe, fum*, my imaginative mind said, skewing one giant man with another, stories of intimidation conjoining and playing hard with this serious moment.

The more he misperceived me the angrier I felt, and I began to inflame red right there. What if I had a gun, what if I had a knife, and we were stuck in such proximity with this anger rising in me? What if I really *was* this person who'd assaulted four police officers and had now felt rejected by my neighborhood homeless shelter, with the threat of detention if I didn't fulfill my service hours? Maybe everywhere I would go I'd meet this same treatment of rejection—it would be a dead end leading to rage and isolation.

His final words shocked me back, though he'd repeated them twice: "If you've assaulted someone, you *cannot* work here," he said dully, the bland eyes, the lips in one flat line across.

I walked away, scared by my anger. I walked back through the kitchen. The kitchen staff turned to me as I passed, and I sputtered "good-bye," not stopping in case the lock in my throat would unlock in front of them. I walked through the double glass doors and stepped between the sprawled men on the stairs, saying nothing. They were not my friends, they would never be faces and names I'd come to know, no one here would be people to me now, nor would I want to drop off goods here again, feeling like part of the community. For even here, even this haven where addicts could find medical support, cold children could find clothes, homeless and hungry folk could find a hot meal, even this place was not my friend.

It began to rain. I crossed Georgia Avenue and continued down the cracked and split-up pavement of Silver Spring Avenue. I opened the broken umbrella in my backpack. It began to pour and the ribs on one side of the umbrella wilted down like my hair. *Soak me*, I thought, walking while wracking-hard sobs propelled me unevenly forward. I walked, I sobbed, I hobbled drunkenly, spouting loud words like the angry street people of my childhood:

This is the slippery slope, this is the path to insanity that starts with being arrested, being framed, a criminal record that gets you fired from your job, the rent you then can't pay, the marriage that falls apart, the kids taken from you, the homelessness, the at-risk as you slip lower and darker with each mean act. Until you lose it altogether.

I sobbed, I ranted. This world was not a world I would live in anymore. No more. Sadness at leaving my children, the damage this would do to them; I sobbed harder, harder, it rained, I sobbed, I walked, it rained, I sobbed—I was soaked through my shoes, my privileged Merrell shoes, my socks Sharon sent me one Christmas, with holes in them but Smartwool nonetheless, and soaked, all this privilege soaked, all belief in goodness of people, all my dad's credos shot, all his optimism, his knowing that right would rule, that "the arc of the moral universe is long but it bends toward justice," as said Martin Luther King, Jr.

No. No. The arc is too goddamn long and I cannot bend with it, I cannot do this alone.

Where was kindness, where was one smile, one belief in me, one person stepping up to protest what never should have happened from the onset of entering my home unannounced? Where was the absolute diehard refusal to accept *any* of this and where were people taking the *action* to go with that refusal. I didn't matter at all. I had not mattered to any one of these people I'd encountered. If I didn't matter, how would people who had no support, no house, no job, survive this entrapment? Even the flurry of reporters and staff who'd circled me after the Community Town Hall Meeting with the County Executive had petered out to nothing, no action, no follow up. "We can't address a case while it's under investigation," County Executive Isaiah Leggett's office staff eventually told me when I called eight times to follow up on their purported interest to meet with me. Perhaps they'd have given attention to the issue if I'd died? *Was it necessary to die?*

My rage was a turn-off. To everyone. Was my rage also my fault? Even the lawyer's weird words, "You're not a victim, you know. You'll get over this," made me angry. Sure, he'd cleared me of a criminal record and much agitation—why wasn't I dancing a jig? Maybe because I hadn't deserved the jail threat and the harm done to me in the first place. And what rankled to a sobering degree was that I'd had to remind him weekly to attend to my case, comparatively unimportant and unprofitable. He'd even showed up at the wrong courthouse on my court date. My husband's cousin, a lawyer, had tactfully intervened to keep him on our case.

"Go into silence," my body said.

Go into silence.

Silence was a place I'd gone on occasion with my kids, when I felt that I might lash out from frustration and exhaustion. Perhaps once every couple of years I'd write them a note that said I was going into silence for the rest of the afternoon. Here was a safer place where my words would have to be written, a thoughtful process; or I would use sign language, which I loved and wanted my kids to learn. Some clarity and power returned through silence.

But I wanted my neighbors to know what had happened—now that my case was expunged and I could speak, I wanted both silence to calm my suicidal thoughts, and a huge noisy uprising to protest what had happened. I walked wet with the rain beating and cold, but my head was organizing now, finding creative mouse holes to creep through to another side. A little bit of light was showing, vague light, the light you see that is blindingly bright yet so tiny, and at a moment in time you are so desperate for that light, any light.

The Silent Vigil was borne at that moment in that rain on that walk. It was an epiphany, the voice of wisdom beyond myself. It was godsend. It was action birthed within the narrow walls allowed me. This was the swell of creativity that sometimes surges up from desperation and helps one activate enough to live. There was no experiential template of a previous silent vigil for me to follow. But perhaps it was a deep reach and revamp of the peace marches we were constantly dragged to as children. Or perhaps it was a mental medley of childhood peace marches and adult AIDS marches, candles held in our mittens as we walked the quilt's perimeter. Some amalgamation erupted in new form within me, my savior arriving at that desperate, precipice moment.

It was late December for the Silent Vigils, temperatures in the 20's and 30's and often raining. Five vigils were held in silence from 8:00 p.m. to just after 11:00 p.m., marking the time when our fateful barbecue had started to the time after I was handcuffed and carted away.

Dear Neighbors, Friends, Family, Colleagues,

After much pain and soul-searching, we begin a silent vigil in our Silver Spring neighborhood on Friday night Dec 27 from 8:00 p.m. to 11:20 p.m. The purpose of this gathering is to acknowledge the complexity of hurt and rage between citizens and police, and to recognize both as capable of intelligent, compassionate human connection.

On Hallowe'en night, a confluence of unfortunate circumstances occurred nearby, and the end result was that I was tackled by the police in the alley outside our backyard, wrestled to the ground, handcuffed, and taken to jail. It has been a brutal and eye-opening experience for me and my family. Suddenly, I was in danger of being found guilty for any of four charges on a police report filled with falsehoods. While Ferguson and Garner were our national experience, I learned firsthand how powerlessness begets powerlessness, and had I not the basic supports of a job, a home, and the good fortune of mental health, education, family, and a myriad of other advantages, the event would have destroyed me.

*As it is, my rage is potentially destructive, and it is this
that must be turned into good use if I am not to mirror the
hostility we faced in the police. Although we are actively
working on policy reforms, attitude also must change:
Human beings being humane. The silent vigil allows me,
and anyone who cares to join, the time to return to quiet
strength and wisdom as we move toward change.*

I strung a light on the fence in the alley, and made an overhang
with a tarp, under which I posted a long scroll of paper with
the headline, *WORLD: I SPOKE OUT IN SILENCE.* Waterproof
markers hung from strings for people to sign their names.
Neighbors who saw my email on the listserv came in winter jackets
and raincoats, umbrellas and boots, their gloved hands fumbling
in bags for reading glasses. They shared flashlights and read my
typed description of what had happened and why I was in silence.
Their faces were serious as they came and went, their comments
in the comment book heartfelt: Dori, Lora, Ethan, Deborah, Tom,
Helen, Carol and Mark, Christine and Auggie, Vicki and her kids
Nathan, Jeremy and Mariana; Mae, Annie, Evie, Gene, Mark P.,
Mark S., Lisa, Melissa and son Jack, Cathy K., Kathie B., Nadja
and Julep.

And Mary. On January 3, the last, coldest, nastiest raining
night when only three people came, a woman emerged from the
dark street, literally a lit face entering my alley. She was my cousin
Jane's friend, a woman I'd never met before but whose presence
made me cry immediately, though she was nearly hidden under
rain gear, her hood cinched so that only the tiniest inner circle of
a kind face was seen. She was Mary Hunt, feminist theologian and

co-founder of WATER—Women's Alliance for Theology, Ethics and Ritual—and the strength and power in her expression was worth the discomfort of those wet and cold hours. Like my cousin Jane's solidarity email, *Stay with the allies,* Mary's face in the rain was a drink of strength serum, the silent arrival of an advocate, an activist, a social justice angel, to my alley.

Action helped. Action helps. No one rose to action beyond my alley; that is to say, no follow-up came from the Silent Vigils. That hurt; it perpetuated my sense of isolation. But at least I had acted, not with suicidal action, but with trying again to reach out. Creating. Believing. It didn't change anything. But it kept me going one more week.

Each meaningful action matters.

Each meaningful action matters. I remember the negative email responses suggesting I take my posts elsewhere. But I also remember each face that turned up on each cold night that I held the vigil.

I remember my friend Carol reading the comments book and writing in it, then going back to her house to get another pair of socks. She sat on a makeshift bench during a sub-freezing Silent Vigil, the two of us huddled under a fleece, unspeaking, occasionally writing a word or two. Nearly no one came the rest of that night it was so cold. But there was my friend Carol seated beside me.

CHAPTER 4

The Social Worker

Distinct from psychopathology,
moral injury is a normal human response
to an abnormal traumatic event.

—RITA NAKASHIMA BROCK

THE SOCIAL WORKER

THE SOCIAL WORKER (TSW) WAS the best dressed of us and the least put out, for she knew why she was in the cell and what it would take to go home. She'd been driving from a party when she was pulled over and arrested, arriving in our cell as if she'd scored nice clothes at Chico's before joining our motley crew.

Her sweater-blouse pullover was black with sparkly circles. I remember the shine like stars in a black night. Her pants were black polyester with neat creases down the front. She seemed perhaps Italian American, dark hair, olive skin, about my height—5'8"—and probably thirty-seven years old.

TSW was down-to-earth. Not rich, not poor, not saving the world, not ignoring it. Not above an arrest, not a criminal, not okay about being here, but not particularly distressed.

It was an It Could Happen To You, story. There were speeding tickets—too many. A new speed camera had been erected along her driving path between home and social work job, and she hadn't noticed. Tickets began arriving in the mail and before she knew it, she had more than she could pay. After Washington DC rent and expenses, who had an *extra $300 for fines? She stalled. The tickets accrued charges on top of original fees—should she borrow the money from her mom? Too much shame. An envelope arrived with a summons to appear in court, but she never opened it.*

Police car lights flashed, and an officer pulled The Social Worker over on this Hallowe'en night. Something had drawn his attention to her car, and when the officer ran her license through the computer, he saw her flagrant past and booked her.

She arrived clean, her shoulder-length hair neatly combed, her face a little strained but not overly so. I doubt she thinks about that night except to pay her tickets one at a time when they arrive through her mail slot.

True, I had fished for her story. Sometimes it comforts me to think about the other guy when I'm in great distress, and so I did with each cellmate. As a young reporter, I discovered that interviewing someone dropped me into an embodied zone that combatted my shyness, made me unselfconscious. I could do it at a party, too, and dissolve the lump in my throat, the awkwardness of my long limbs. Turning the tables to ask someone about themselves was a natural survival tool I'd later see substantiated in scientific data: caring about or helping another can occupy a struggling mind and give it healthy focus. This increases oxytocin levels and, the study showed, life span. More to the point, I learned facts about my cellmates this way, and the exchange of our words connected us deeply. But the tables did turn—as they had with Baby—and The Social Worker, who I aptly named for her vocation, clearly had her eyes out for my "case."

"What are your charges?" she asked.

I said I didn't know.

"They're written on your papers," she said.

I looked at her blankly. What papers?

She nodded to the wad I was clutching. I hadn't noticed I'd been rolling and twisting something, nor did I remember receiving the papers, now a tighter and tighter cylinder spinning in my fists. I untwirled the springform and tried to make out the blur of words. My scraping vision was like seeing through scratchy cotton wool, plus at age sixty...

"Would you like me to read them to you?" she asked, after watching me study the page.

I looked at her face. How did she see that I couldn't see? Her expression was neutral and non-condescending: it would be a factual read, and hopefully not too loud.

I handed her my papers in faith.

As I write this, I remember how she felt bigger than me. She was whole in her body whereas I had left mine. I barely filled my skin. Though tension had bloated my stomach so that I craved to lay belly-down on the concrete floor, the rest of me had no fullness, no rapture to be alive, only the grey outline of my body in this black and white box. I became as small while standing as I could.

What she would read to me was startling. And seemed so private, I wanted to shush her voice. How would other cellmates perceive me if they heard such charges? Would they not see me as me, just like the police had not? Would they judge me solely by what they heard The Social Worker read out loud?

Would my cellmates question my mental health as the bully cop had implied? Would they sneak looks at my irises to see if they were dilated, like the first cop shining his flashlight in my eyes? Who was who here? Who was I to them? Was I safe in this room?

In the months that followed this night I felt the frailty of my mind. A schism had occurred that I can best describe this way: What I'd seen about our system was more than I could integrate. What had physically happened to me was more shocking than I could absorb. And this: When an assaulter lies to cover up his actions, it triples the psychosocial damage to the victim.

As the Social Worker read on, the timbre of the officers' claims, the tone of falsehood and meanness, hit home like the slam after slam of the metal cell door. I slumped onto the bench. Our home had been violated, my body violated, I was under arrest, and now the police who'd assaulted me re-framed the truth and stuck it to me with criminal charges.

Oh.

Those papers.

This is how it works.

Welcome to America!

Perhaps I got it at that moment that a history bigger than mine had erupted at my gate. Perhaps I knew already that it would take forever to recover—if "recovery" was the aim.

I felt very alone then, and for a long time to follow. Though I needn't have. Plenty of folk had been a harsher version of this road before me, including my own kin.

WHY DIDN'T I GO SEE a therapist?

Let's start here. I have a certain irritation that, in our society, any time someone sheds tears or a story of pain, inevitably comes the suggestion to seek therapy.

We have pathologized life.

Life has super painful twists. Super twisting pains. Painful, super-twisted shit happens. You get the point.

I'm not against therapy. I'm a yoga therapist, for goodness sake, and much of what we do in yoga therapy is to be patient with the physical manifestations of emotional pain that have been swept under a trapezius muscle, into a bloodstream, into a heart's rhythm, into tension in the joints. We wait it out and then dive in with kindness. It shocks the system over and over to receive compassionate touch, guidance in movements that strengthen or release, and an ear—most importantly—that truly listens, accompanied by eyes that put the person in front of them first.

It's basic.

It takes a lifetime to learn.

So, why didn't I go to someone who could do the above? Well, it was complicated, though I did practice in a form that's the next best thing and was already part of my routine. Every other Saturday, I met with my old co-counseling buddy, Betty, usually at my house, sequestered in our attic. I'd have chairs arranged for us, a timer, and a box of tissues. Though I seemed to never have that box of tissues, so it was napkins, or a roll of toilet paper, I admit.

We prepped bolsters of several sizes before we started. I used them to smack out some of the rage.

Re-evaluation Counseling, or RC, is an international institution that isn't very institutionalized. Some folks complain about that. But I find it appealing. It's grassroots. The premise, in my words, is simple: You've got some shit covering up the clarity. Get rid of some of the shit so you can thrive on that clarity. It's like the cloud cover I see out the window as I type this.

The load of pain we carry is the cloud cover. We clear it in a number of ways. For me, some of those are what you see here. Expression through creativity. Speaking through writing, through movement, through art and song.

Or we clear it by telling our heart's story, by weeping it out, by laughing about it if possible, therefore contradicting the stronghold of pain, and by yawning to release the clutch it has on us. We break the grip of fear that could later become us or in the past paralyzed us, by shaking it through and *off* our bodies—a natural mammalian practice. In the presence of a kind and attentive listener, the cloud cover gradually thins and becomes more vaporous as we discharge terrifying memory. Afterwards, whether raging about the violence of police on our body, or weeping for feelings of failure as a parent, we can see the valley now below. Then when we have to deal with that valley, the view is clear; and our *actions* come from a power that is non-malevolent.

So I co-counseled with Betty—free of charge of course, for we turned the stubborn timer for thirty to fifty-five minutes each way, taking turns as counselor, turns as client. For this co-counseling, for Betty my lifesaver, I am thankful.

But I'm a yoga therapist. Where were the yoga therapists I so needed? The Phoenix Rising Yoga Therapists near me had retired. They told me so in surprisingly clipped emails that offered neither solace nor direction.

Really? How cold of them. I pause while editing this and dig back five years through my emails, one in particular from my former boss, a prominent yoga studio owner who first introduced me to yoga therapy twenty-five years ago, before it was trendy. Her email is kind and she apologizes that she's no longer available for this work, offering the name of someone who does good bodywork related to trauma and healing. She wishes me well over and over and sends love.

Yet I remembered it as a "clipped email that offered neither solace nor direction." At the time, it was another slammed door, a door I'd hoped had a welcoming practitioner with helping hands on the other side. What I now register as kind words I read then as rejection, another person who didn't believe me, didn't understand, or didn't want to work with me.

And my emails to her were written carefully so that I didn't sound too desperate; too falling over the edge; too much about to jump off; too losing my shit.

Oh.

The active Phoenix Rising Yoga Therapists nearest to me were an hour's drive to somewhere I hadn't been, involving the Capital Beltway and freeways I couldn't drive in my traumatized state. And I didn't know if these practitioners were seasoned enough for what I needed. One African American practitioner was both a clinical social worker and a Phoenix Rising Yoga Therapist with a background in trauma work. I contacted her but couldn't stomach the two-hour drive.

I was in a Master of Science graduate program for Yoga Therapy. You'd have thought I'd have plenty of yoga therapy practitioners to choose from. But no, I felt they were being trained in posttraumatic stress techniques and I wasn't confident that anyone understood the critical state of *active* trauma I was in. There was nothing "post" about it. I was deep in the *now* of an assault to my light, to my body, to my faith, to my mental state, to my family, to my finances, and to my future if the police charges against me won in court. *Please don't ask me to do breathing practices. Please don't suggest restorative poses with my eyes closed and my body vulnerable.* Were we being trained to work with victims of police assault? Certainly not. I would have to make up this training myself.

But what about speaking with a counselor, or a psychotherapist, or someone trained in Somatic Experiencing? Great ideas, and there are so many modalities. How about EMDR? Neuro-linguistic Reprogramming? Brainspotting and others, too many to list. Had I a relationship with such a practitioner, no doubt I would have continued with enthusiasm to see her. But I did not. I had a rapport established with Betty, so it was Betty's ear I bent, Betty holding the bolster I beat, Betty holding my hand as I wretched up bile, pain, fury, fear. Betty's presence kept me this side of sanity. A quote from David Brooks' *New York Times* article, "The Art of Presence," describes what Betty and I orchestrated; and it describes what I longed for from friends and family but seemed too much to ask in busy times:

> *Grant the sufferers the dignity of their own process. Let them define meaning.*

> *Sit simply through moments of pain and uncomfortable darkness.*

Then a therapist friend sent me a list of Somatic Experiencing practitioners. I considered the list, studying each bio like I was seeking a life partner. Beyond expense, logistics, and stranger phobia, the nagging, irrefutable question loomed: who would understand *this* somatic experience, this body shock—what therapists, with all their skilled knowledge of loss and grief and trauma, had any experience with police assault?

Can we just say it?

What white practitioner was going to get this?

Of course any good therapist could have lent useful council, but I did not know a good one and the process of finding one was way beyond my current problem-solving capacity—and my trust of strangers. I barely trusted the people I knew, for they were thrown left and right in reaction to this tale.

There was the issue of money as well. We had my grad school expenses and my older son's college fees, we had little health insurance and no mental health coverage, and the charge I saw listed for one-on-one therapy was at minimum $185. I visited one somatic practitioner's group class for trauma survivors, where I could check her out for a fraction of the cost of private care. Her ad for "safe, guided movement" sounded great. The class met just five minutes from me, and with relative ease I parked and found the entrance to the mammoth office building. But the calming body practices based on tai chi didn't speak to my isolating rage, and when I left, the elevator doors opened to a different exit from where I'd entered. I became lost in the maze of vacant, echoing halls, and each time I found an exit, I couldn't find my car. My heart raced to a frightening beat and my face inflamed hot/cold, red welts forming down my neck—it was almost dark, *I had to be home before dark to be safe.* Fortunately, as I waited for the elevator to retrace my steps to the therapy room, the doors opened and the teacher herself came out. She led me back to "start" and to the right exit for my car. I jumped in, locked the doors, and sped home as if bad guys were chasing me.

Did I need a prescription?

Let me say this. If I were a drinker, I'd have picked up the speed with drink. If I were a smoker, tobacco, pot, I would have smoked all day. If I were a pill popper, I'd have visited my dealer or my doc and stocked up. But I have an aversion to most recreational drugs, and even coffee is too high a high for my system. Others in my position probably would have been prescribed some happy pill to help the dark nights and the dim days. I didn't want to explain myself to a prescriber; I didn't want a confluence of tears and emotional wrenching in someone's therapy room to elicit a prescribed invitation, *just to get you through this period.*

Am I masochistic? Perhaps. I know this: When my hair turned grey I wasn't thrilled, but I wanted to see how it would happen. Would it be an asymmetrical stripe like a cockeyed skunk, or would it be flecks of sparkle around the edges? I was curious. If I colored it, which concerned me for toxicity, I'd never know *how* the change had occurred, nor if I liked it. Then I'd be stuck with dying my head until one radical day (age 70? 85? 90?—when would I say *basta*?) when I'd let it go white and shock myself, among others. I'm the weird patient who goes for a blood test and watches the nurse put the needle in my arm; I never look away.

On a graver note, the police assault was my new reality, and I needed to know how to live with it. *How would I recover sanity? What was I meant to learn—to DO? How on earth would I integrate this experience into my life and how in heaven could I come out healthy?*

The latter is still a question. As I type this, I swipe my forehead, my ears, my left brow, all of them reddened still, the skin like a burn victim's. I know it's chemical overload. I know I can only control so much of this. The aftermath, two years after the assault, still seems beyond my scope to control. Hair falls out, my ears are swollen; a rash still forms a perfect 6-inch circle on my left ribs. I walk up and down stairs in the style of a toddler, my knees in pain.

It's sad to me that all my work, re-focus, and emotional discharge of hurt can't eradicate the symptoms. It's sadder yet that all my efforts to self-heal—even if successful—can't cure the historical patterns of dominance and police aggression that underlie this assault that brought on the onset of my symptoms. This is my *nation's* problem. What good is *feel better and forget?*

Therapy, as I see it, is the creative expression through writing this book, the active speaking out for police reform, the marching with women who lost their sons to police violence, the healing through self-prescribed yoga, the discharge of poison with Betty, the helping of other trauma victims, and then the compassion meditations where, finally after many months, even the most bully assaulter is sent my words borrowed from a Buddhist loving-kindness prayer:

May you be happy
May you be healthy
May you be peaceful
May you live your life with ease

I weep to repeat these words. I proofread them, and it storms again. Compassion for those who've harmed us requires a gestation period—time—before one can even give it thought. Eventually, miraculously, though the chant brings up pain and bile, it is a relief to attempt to speak soul to soul. Police are people, with mothers and babies and maybe even a pet at home. Then anger surfaces again over a triggered memory or a parallel news story, and I have to be honest with that, too. *I am up against an entire system.* Can't hold the terror in, can't hold the rage. Release the cloud cover. Then cycle again to compassion. Do this 8,659 times.

An assault reveals dark truths about our society. In this case, it reveals that the current style of policing stimulates hyper-activation in officers, which leads to reactivity. It reveals that U.S. law enforcement harbors a frightening number of unbalanced individuals suffering from PTSD—from military deployment, from distressing experiences on the job, and/or from traumas of earlier, personal past. It reveals that any human, but especially a person of color, can find themselves at the pointed end of an over-reactive officer's gun. In the context of our multi-ethnic middle-class neighborhood, six out of seven law enforcement officers behaved like they were sword-wielding crusaders conquering the infidel, though they were in the infidel's backyard.

I have never been a police officer. But I have heard personal stories of crippling physical and emotional pain, and I worked in the intimacy of a session with a prison warden who suffered both—he'd been jumped by an inmate and had searing back pain, debilitating migraines, and related depression. Seeing a child die on the job is up there as one of the highest stressors, according to my instructors at the Montgomery County CERT (Community Emergency Response Team), with whom I also trained. But surely, every chase, every investigation—all the more so at night as this one was, *and* on the ever-tricky Hallowe'en—is a temptation to attack first and think later.

The most prevalent point surfaced in my mind within seconds of the assault on this night: *What if I was not English speaking?*

What if, like the bully cop implied, I had been drinking? What if I was mentally ill? What if I was a teen? What if my skin-color was brown? My son and his white friend insisted on accompanying their Black friend to his car because my son had seen "dodgy kids" in the park and didn't want his pal to walk solo. Not because he'd have to protect him from the *police.* He'd sniffed trouble from these youth, who indeed, proved trouble.

But my three kids were assumed to be those dangerous youth, and the police followed them: first an elderly plain-clothed policeman who thought he'd found the perpetrators of a local assault, then the back-up officers in squad cars who dove into my backyard, pulled out my kids, and were interrogating them when I appeared. *Did they notice they'd just broken into someone's home?* I introduced myself repeatedly, thinking they hadn't heard correctly because they were forcing me back into my own gate.

Here's the bottom line—it is the sensory experience that informed me most accurately within seconds of my arrival on the scene: the first police officers I encountered showed symptoms of sympathetic nervous system arousal. Their eyes looked—in straight-forward language—freaky, huge, glaring. Their faces were frozen, their voices monotone and mean. *No ventral vagal innervation,* research tells me; there was an absence of the kind of facial expression that engages with other humans and results in successful social communication. The brain's tenth cranial nerve, the *vagus nerve,* through attachments to striated muscles of the face and vocal chords, *and* the muscles of our heart and gut, literally messages our nervous system to be sounded in our voice and written on our faces. "In a sense we're wearing our heart on our face," says neuroscientist Stephen Porges.

I can see them as if they're in front of me now, faces that still frighten me as I recall the disconnect in their eyes, the set of their mouths, the combativeness of their postures bullying me back, and their high beam light held to my eyes, blinding me.

Were they checking *my* irises for drug use?

The fact that I was the Mom, the homeowner, and in charge of these minors, was of no interest to them—none of the traits of *mother, elder, lawful citizen*, that might have positively filtered into their prejudices affected the faces I encountered.

Should we be worried about this? Yes and no. One can see that this was not a case of racial profiling. But if their reactions had nothing to do with ethnicity, skin color, gender, or age, how do we *name* the assault and criminal framing that happened?

As I'm re-writing the introduction to this book, I google "black professor stopped by the police while walking." I am looking for the name of a woman with whom I felt deep sisterhood and about whom I wrote many pages on scratch paper I can't find. I'd read about her in a news story in 2015: *Dorothy Bland*, a professor at the University of North Texas.

Professor Bland, (no relationship to *Sandra* Bland, who died in police custody), was at home one day, got up from her computer after hours of academic work and decided to take a walk even though it was raining. Exercise is good for clearing the mind, re-setting the breath, staving off diabetes, high blood pressure and weight gain—all the docs say this.

She's walking in her suburban Dallas neighborhood and strolls from the confines of the sidewalk into the near-empty street. It's raining, she has her hood up. From the back, the inexperienced eye decides she's a young Black male in a hooded sweatshirt. Never mind the front says Boston—where she completed the Harvard University Institute for Management and

Leadership in Education — from the back, "he" is flapping arms, "he" must be crazy.

When I watch the dash-cam video as the cop car follows her, here's what I see: A woman (bobby socks and black leggings) getting great cardio and letting off steam by lyrically moving her arms like an eagle in flight. This is how I let myself go too...I walk and flap or push the air—or at least this is what I do when I don't think I'm being watched. Some of us are dancers, artists, movers, expressive human beings; we are not all holed up in our own straightjackets of square and linear movements—some of us love to move! Professor Dorothy Bland, Dean of the School of Journalism at UNT, was not only "walking while Black," she was walking while letting the sun shine into her body through the rain, she was walking while clearing her heart from negative thought and hard work that can make us stale. She was walking *free*. That she was deemed a threat angers me so, I have no words. The police were decent in tone, and they never laid a hand on her, but the mere confrontation of cops asking her not to jaywalk and asking for ID *in her own neighborhood* was terrifying: an insult. And how did the neighbors' racist calls to 911 and the hate posts she received after speaking of this indignance on Facebook (amid shouts to fire her) damage her *spirit* and remind others to bottle the fuck up?

When I google "Black professor stopped by police" to recall her name and check my facts, *there are too many Google hits*—I wade through overwhelming numbers of assaults on Black professors to find Dorothy Bland.

There is video of a different professor, Professor of English Ersula Ore in Arizona: a click sees her accused of jaywalking and violently twirled and slammed to the ground by a campus police officer when she is walking in the street to avoid construction. She had just finished teaching a class and was headed to her car. The officer was put on leave from the university police department, but two years later we see he is a deputy in the next county's sheriff's office.

A search shows that English Professor Ore is still at the same university, but now she's the Lincoln Professor of Ethics in the School of Social Transformation and assistant professor of African and African American Studies and Rhetoric. Her book published in 2019 is titled *"Lynching: Violence, Rhetoric, and American Identity."* I long to speak to her personally, find out about her life trajectory since the assault. But we can deduce plenty from the work shift we see and from knowing this: Five years ago, as a consequence of this police assault, *she* was punished with nine months of probation—*for resisting arrest*. On why she was not more compliant with "an officer touching me and violating me," a cop who threatened he'd slam her on the hood of his car as he arrested her, she wrote 18 months later:

> *My name is Ersula Jawanna Ore, and I'm the one who told a white man with a badge and a gun to go fuck himself... all the while knowing that black bodies enacting self-respect and civic personhood end up hanging from trees, raped, jailed, murdered in jail, and dead in the streets ... I am still not whole, still not healed, but I am, unlike so many others, still alive.*

Then I read artist Steve Locke's post, the Massachusetts art professor detained by cops on his way to teach his 1:30 class. He had stopped to get a burrito—while Black—wearing a hand-knitted cap and a brown jacket; and when the police say he is a suspect in a just-reported crime and they're taking him in to be identified:

It was at this moment that I knew that I was probably going to die. I am not being dramatic when I say this. I was not going to get into a police car. I was not going to present myself to some victim. I was not going let someone tell the cops that I was not guilty when I already told them that I had nothing to do with any robbery. I was not going to let them take me anywhere because if they did, the chance I was going to be accused of something I did not do rose exponentially. I knew this in my heart. I was not going anywhere with these cops and I was not going to let some white woman decide whether or not I was a criminal, especially after I told them that I was not a criminal. This meant that I was going to resist arrest. This meant that I was not going to let the police put their hands on me.

Something weird happens when you are on the street being detained by the police. People look at you like you are a criminal. The police are detaining you so clearly you must have done something, otherwise they wouldn't have you. No one made eye contact with me. I was hoping that someone I knew would walk down the street or come out of one of the shops or get off the 39 bus or come out of JP Licks and say to these cops, "That's Steve Locke. What the FUCK are you detaining him for?"

By the time I've found Dorothy Bland's name and refreshed my knowledge of her police stop, I am sobbing from this nauseating revisit to police abuse. Not one of these people was in any altercation—nor even in a threatening circumstance—at the time of their arrest or near-arrest. Two of them were women. All of them were professors; all of them walking with a destination; two of them in broad daylight; all of them Black.

But why am I surprised and horrified? I was raised during the violent civil rights era when police assaults upon multitudes in the South were finally captured by press and TV crews—police using dogs, bayonets, tear gas, hoses, guns, and clubs upon peaceful citizens, elders, clergy in robes, women with children.

I was six months old when Rosa Parks claimed a seat at the front of a bus and I was thirteen when my entire middle school petitioned to change our school's name to Martin Luther King Jr. High, following the horrible, hope-crushing, gut punch of Dr. King's assassination.

I was ten when footage showed Selma, Alabama cops with water hoses, whips, and nightsticks attacking and trampling protestors, and the famous photo of Amelia Boynton beaten on neck and shoulders, tear-gassed and left for dead when police on foot and horseback attacked peaceful marchers and her photo went to international presses, the equivalent of viral. Young organizer, John Lewis, was bludgeoned with a billy club that day on the Edmund Pettus Bridge, his skull fractured; he would later become a Congressman. Organizer Amelia Boynton Robinson lived to be 104 and never stopped fighting—this was the generation that mentored mine.

What most people don't know is that it was ruthless police brutality three weeks prior to that Sunday that spawned the famous voting rights marches. In the small town of Marion, Alabama, five hundred unarmed marchers were singing hymns with the plan to walk to the county jail in solidarity with a civil rights activist held there, then return to their church. Law enforcement shot out streetlights, chased and beat the marchers. Jimmie Lee Jackson, a young deacon, was shot and then clubbed to death by state troopers. He had jumped to the aid of his mother who was being beaten as she tried to defend her father, age eighty-one, who, himself, was being beaten. United Press and NBC news correspondents were also brutally clubbed, their cameras smashed. The Reverend Dr. Martin Luther King, Jr. paid tribute to twenty-seven-year-old Jackson as he was buried—in an old slave burial ground next to his father.

Fury was fueled—and was harnessed into bigger action. A 54-mile march was organized from Selma to the State Capitol in Montgomery. The night of March 7, 1965, ABC news interrupted TV shows in my hometown of Cleveland, showing the graphic footage of the horrors inflicted upon Lewis, Boynton, and hundreds of peaceful protestors as they marched to commemorate Jimmie Lee Jackson and demand voting rights and equality for Black Americans. *Bloody Sunday,* it was called.

The Reverend Martin Luther King, Jr. called upon clergy and lay leaders, who flocked to Selma for a second march; and rallies and demonstrations erupted in eighty U.S. cities. Members of our progressive community in Cleveland organized local support. Some bused to Selma. *Turnaround Tuesday,* the second Selma-to-Montgomery march was named, after Dr. King held a short prayer session on the Edmund Pettus Bridge, and then, to obey a federal injunction, safely turned the several thousand marchers around.

That night, three white Unitarian Universalist ministers were attacked. They were beaten by white segregationists as they left an integrated café. James Reeb, a UU minister from Boston, thirty-seven years old and the father of four, who lived and worked with poor communities, died from brain injuries: the local Black hospital wasn't equipped to help him and the white hospital wouldn't take him.

Busloads of ministers, priests, rabbis, and social activists arrived from around the country for a third march—they were protected by 1,900 Alabama National Guard and FBI Marshals, ordered by President Lyndon Johnson against the will of segregationist Governor George Wallace. Some activists marched for three days, sleeping in the fields of Black farmers at night. Others arrived to show solidarity at the end. They were perhaps 50,000-strong at the last stretch, including our busloads from Cleveland, arm in arm across the wide swath of road. Rosa Parks, Reverend Ralph Abernathy, Dr. King, and the revered Coretta Scott King, marched at the helm, followed by thousands, tired and united, in song.

While this was the televised terror of the South and the great victory of the Voting Rights Act that followed, we were a Northern family, and our weekend civil rights marches were peaceful—celebrities like world-renown pediatrician Dr. Benjamin Spock marched beside us. Sunday gatherings were collating parties to put out newsletters for peace and freedom—sticky Danish coffee cakes, Sara Lee pound cake, mimeographed pages we kids folded into perfect thirds as we stood in assembly lines ending with envelopes to lick. People were kind and purposeful, integrated picnics were fun and worry-free, and the only threatening moment I registered was when we lost our dad during a fundraiser and had to jungle through adult thighs till his laugh radared us to find him.

But there was more. He was jailed overnight when he integrated a local swimming pool with his friend, Thurmond. There were FBI raids, our close friends were jailed for one year—information kept from us but for the exciting news that their daughter, our pal Lucy, almost came to live in our apartment—another sister! Ethel and Julius Rosenberg had been executed by electric chair in Sing Sing, and no one knew who was next: our mom and dad were subpoenaed to appear before HUAC, the House Un-American Committee, in 1954 and 1955. My father had helped lead the national campaign to Save the Rosenbergs; my mother, the one college graduate in her family and the first woman reporter to cover The White House, was now a leader with the Women's International League for Peace and Freedom and the Cleveland Committee to Secure Justice in the Rosenberg Case. The punishing McCarthy Era targeted civil rights leaders along with Hollywood actors, academics, and labor-union leaders; and it dealt a hammer blow to the movement for Black equality, delaying the fall of Jim Crow segregation laws. I was a newborn with two sisters, and while I always knew I'd inherited some attitude from my father, now I see the verve and audacity of my mother—her gumption, fortitude, belligerence, and refusal to name names even in the face of mortal danger as she sat alone through interrogations by HUAC's chief investigators:

Mr. TAVENNER.   What is your middle initial?

Mrs. ROTHENBERG. My middle initial is "S."

Mr. TAVENNER.   M.S., then, M. S. would be
                      the proper initials to
                      represent your name; is
                      that correct?

Mrs. ROTHENBERG. Presumably.

Mr. TAVENNER.   Presumably?

Mrs. ROTHENBERG. Presumably, if one's
                      name were—

Mr. FORER.   A very cute observation.

Mr. TAVENNER.   Here is another article from
                      the Plain Dealer which will
                      be more specific as to the
                      name. It bears a date of
                      June 14, 1953:

                      *"37 en route to appeal for
                      spies, many left-wingers
                      board bus to Washington."*

                      You didn't go to Washington,
                      did you, with the group?

Mrs. ROTHENBERG. I decline to answer for the same reason. I believe the story does say that a Mrs. Don Rothenberg did not board the bus; it said she had to stay home with her children.

Mr. TAVENNER. Is that correct?

Mrs. ROTHENBERG. I decline to answer.

Mr. TAVENNER. You are not willing to state anything under oath about it?

Chairman Walter. Of what crime do you think you might be convicted by admitting you stayed home with your children.

Mr. FORER. What crime does she think she is guilty of by staying home with her children?

Mrs. ROTHENBERG. I don't think it is any crime. As a matter of fact, that is where I should be right now.

The HUAC team's fruitless questioning continues until they give up, resigned:

Mr. TAVENNER.   Were you a member of the Communist Party at any time during the year 1953?

Mrs. ROSENBERG.   [note, misspelled name, sic] I decline to answer and invoke my privilege under the fifth amendment.

Mr. TAVENNER.   Are you now a member of the Communist Party?

Mrs. ROTHENBERG.   I am hesitating because I realize the dilemma this kind of questioning leads people into, but I am forced to invoke my privilege under the fifth amendment not to be a witness against myself.

Mr. TAVENNER.   Will you tell the committee what disposition was made by the Cleveland Committee to Secure Justice in the Rosenberg Case, of the funds raised by it for the Rosenberg family?

Mrs. ROTHENBERG. I decline to answer for the reasons stated previously, but if you want a question of opinion, Mr. Counsel, my objective opinion would be that any funds—

Mr. TAVENNER. I am not interested in your opinion. If you have no facts on which you are willing to testify under oath, I am not interested in your opinion. No further questions.

(Whereupon the witness [my mother] was excused.)

Were law enforcement officers friendly people or frightening people? As children we were taught to find a policeman if we needed to know a street address or if we'd lost our dog. But we also saw that police were dangerous—in the South. In the North, policemen stood guard while we marched, and directed traffic. Yet, subterranean things happened: men in uniform could make parents disappear, or wreck people's lives. There were Bad Guys and Good Guys—with the North coming out on top, but disappointingly, that soon began to change.

We moved to Berkeley, California when I was eleven, and after our first day of school, our dad and new stepmother sat waiting in the living room to speak with us—now five kids, soon six. My father had the Berkeley Gazette in hand and grimly held up the front page for us to see his photo. "You're in the paper, Daddy!" I exclaimed, always proud of my well-known dad. He pointed to the headline, the finger-sized letters in bold caps fit for declaration of war: **COMMUNIST COMES TO BERKELEY**. Not coincidentally, the organization that had guaranteed him a 2-year contract, Californians for Liberal Representation, went bust one month later, and my parents who'd just bought a home for what was then an exorbitant $40,000, spiraled into debt.

At my first after-school job as a busboy, my Nazi boss, Robert Rinehart of Rinehart's Hofateria, climbed agitatedly onto the red vinyl bench at the front window and pretended to shoot down Vietnam War protestors, my oldest sister, Linda, among them. "Dirty commie hippies," he growled, making the *eh-eh-eh-eh-eh* sound of his imaginary machine gun as he shot them down. "I wish I had my Uzi."

Yes, Berkeley would introduce me to what I'd always assumed to be a Southern problem, the brutal pitting of law enforcement against citizens. It was the late sixties, a volatile and life-costing time of service overseas and protests at home. At the University of California, Berkeley, students had appropriated a derelict plot of land to build a corner for free speech where they'd be uncensored by campus authorities. Local merchants and residents supported the plan, the University Chancellor promised to notify the committee prior to taking any counteraction, and over 1,000 volunteers cleared rubble and landscaped—planting trees, flowers, shrubs, and laying sod to create "People's Park."

But Governor Reagan, who viewed the campus as "a haven for communist sympathizers, protesters, and sex deviants," had been elected in part for his popular campaign to crack down on campus activism. He overrode the Chancellor's promise that no action would occur without warning and sent in California Highway Patrol and Berkeley police to destroy the park and erect chain link around it. This was met by protests, in turn met with additional troops who shot tear gas and buckshot, hitting bystanders and the backs of protestors as they fled. One man died, one was permanently blinded, three had punctured lungs, one a shattered leg, another a punctured stomach that would bring chronic pain for fifty years—over 128 people were hospitalized, many more treated by teams of medical students.

Bloody Thursday, it was called.

The Sheriff later admitted that some of his deputies—many of them just home from service in Vietnam—had aggressively pursued protestors "as though they were Viet Cong."

To quell the protests, Governor Reagan ordered 2,700 National Guard into our town, and as they barreled up University Blvd past our school each day, my brother Jeff and his clever friend Eric taped dimes and pennies just the right weight to set off the railroad gates, leaving a caravan of armored trucks waiting for a train that never arrived. For two weeks, Berkeley was under martial law, the sky rumbling with helicopters dispensing tear gas that blanketed the entire city, sending school kids miles away to hospitals—perhaps a "tactical mistake," the Governor later conceded, although his instructions had been, "If it takes a bloodbath, let's get it over with." Some National Guardsmen who were ordered to point bayonets and shoot live ammunition at protestors were also students at Berkeley. One UC student who had participated in the protest that week, was shot, got medical treatment, and went to lie down in his dorm room only to find a notice to report for guard duty the next day.

"The US government...authorized the killing of its own (white) children," wrote The Guardian in a book review about the four Kent State deaths the following year and this military nightmare of People's Park.

It was four years after Selma.

What would The Social Worker say? She seemed a pragmatic girl. She might not always pay her bills on time but neither do I—hence I don't keep a Macy's card. She'd have folded one long arm with thumb and forefinger to chin in a pensive gesture, her brown eyes deep. She'd have offered that the heritage of U.S. policing with Southern slave patrols—brutal—and Northern night watchmen—drunk, sleeping, cavorting—wasn't a great foundation and now *it's no wonder*, she would say, though her words wouldn't be filled with emotion. She would state that slave patrols morphed neatly into vigilante groups, begetting the Ku Klux Klan after Confederates lost the Civil War and needed a club. *I guess it was a support group for them*, I'd say, and she would look at me blankly, not sure if I was serious or stupid. *People were lynching people*, she'd say, *victimizing Black people mostly—in the South—but also whites, and in other states, Mexicans, Native Americans, Chinese, Italian, Greek, Jewish, Australians, Finish and Germans—and not just the South; the Midwest, the Southwest, the border states.* In San Francisco, a century before I lived there, the Committee of Vigilance boasted 6,000 members, popular for its "law-enforcement"—lynching, whipping, deportation.

Sticking your nose out by owning land or business as a minority, rising to any position of power—these upward moves made you liable, and if you were white and showed advocacy you were toast. In 1870, a prominent mixed-race constable in North Carolina who'd attempted to protect the Black community from the KKK in his small town, was dragged from bed to be lynched in front of the county courthouse, the words "Beware ye guilty, both white and black" on his chest. A Black man who named the murderers was soon dead in a pond.

I should have kept that in mind: *cops support their own*. By the 1920's the KKK was four million strong, and hoods on or off, white supremacists got away with, literally, murder— targeting immigrants, minorities, labor organizations, and civil rights marchers like those from Selma to Montgomery. In 1965, James Reeb's killers were tried and acquitted in Alabama—by an all-white jury. The State Trooper who shot Jimmie Lee Jackson was transferred to Birmingham where he was promoted.

Our Northern police took a more humane route, right? They weren't animals like the South, where "Klan Courts" stood in for criminal justice. Yet the 1918 anti-lynching bill didn't pass in Congress; nearly 200 bills had been proposed and had failed by 1968; and that anti-lynching law was still floating in August 2020 when these words were typeset. *Sorry, girl,* TSW would say. Or maybe nothing. Maybe she'd just let the silence tell it, that the North had had a good model for policing their big cities in the mid-1800's but blew it.

The nine Peelian Principles, Sir Robert Peel's baby—Britain's former Prime Minister and Home Secretary from whose name the affectionate word *bobbies* comes—provided clear policing guidelines that, (at least initially), influenced U.S. agencies: Wear uniforms so citizens know who you are. Don't carry weapons. Police effectiveness isn't measured by the number of arrests, it's measured by the lack of crime. Trust and accountability are paramount! And Peel's famous words:

"The police are the public and the public are the police."

The Brits carried only batons, adhering to Peel's Principles. But in the melee of bourgeoning U.S. cities, American police began to carry their own firearms. After a New York City police officer killed a weaponless man running from him, the cop was exonerated, and a trend was set. Soon enough, against public outcry, police were issued guns.

It was a field day of corruption: Northern police soon climbed in bed not only with politicians who they ruthlessly protected in exchange for job appointments, but with organized crime. White youth gangs and cops were the enforcers of election fraud, terrorizing union organizers, "foreigners," Catholics, and Blacks, in return for which they earned a friendly nod to the use of force and the win-win of bribes. *Is it always minorities and the property-less who are persecuted rather than protected?* I, a homeowner, would ask The Social Worker. And she'd be silent, letting the question hang.

Only later would she whisper this recent stat that highlights oppression's pattern: *a 2017 CDC study showed that Native Americans are more likely to be killed by police than any other racial or ethnic group.*

In 2006, the FBI Counterterrorism Division published an assessment, *White Supremacist Infiltration of Law Enforcement.* Apparently, it was unheeded. Because recently, The Plain View Project unearthed thousands of racist and vitriolic social media posts from police in eight departments around the country. "It's a good day for a chokehold," was a post from a prolific Phoenix,

Arizona cop. He also posted how he would sexually assault law breakers, which elicited thumbs up from twenty-four other officers. In a trifecta of prejudice, the same officer posted a 2011 meme of a cop in full riot gear at the University of California, Davis, blasting pepper spray directly on the faces of youth seated beneath him in peaceful protest. "Don't mind me," the text reads: "Just watering my hippies."

I would tell TSW this one-stop shopping is handy—to me— for understanding our country's two congruent history plays, South *and* North: how police still exercise corporal punishment like vintage slave patrols and civil rights haters. How this bullshit collided in my backyard with my own history play. How the racist South and corrupt (and racist) North flashed through my gates with their common-law child star, *violence—ta-da!*

I would tell her how this violence was like a torch catching everything to flame, and how the sight of my son in their hands, torched me too.

I would say this if I understood any of it just yet.

And I would tell her, finally, how law enforcement officers can be branded weak, wacko, or disloyal if they complain. She might know that cops can't show their cards of pain or distress, but she might not know how mental health can be used as a trap, and I should tell her. After New York Police Department officer Adrian Schoolcraft, who is white, tape-recorded corruption in the force—including false arrests to make quota, and underreporting crimes such as rape—NYPD cops (led by the deputy chief), broke into Schoolcraft's apartment, dragged him from bed, and committed him to a psych ward where he was handcuffed to a hospital bed and prevented from using a telephone, by orders of police on guard.

This was 2010.

Four years later, when the lawyer I hire to help with my criminal charges tells me I'd better be quiet or I could end up serving time, Schoolcraft's trial outcome is still up in the air. Eric Garner, Michael Brown, and Tamir Rice have just been killed. The brotherhood of the police is tight and shows up right here right now as The Social Worker reads my charges in her loud, clear, blame-free voice: I've assaulted four cops.

The officers in my case were: 2 white males, 3 black males, 1 white female, 1 black female.

They were perhaps in their thirties, early forties.

Only one officer was older. Bald.

Only his eyes totally connected. I had no concern when I saw him talking with two of the teens. He was someone I could have easily spoken to, and from whom I'd expect a communicative response. He was all there. His parasympathetic nervous system was functioning well, his *social engagement system* working. His eyes, I could see more quickly than I can type this now, connected. I am grappling for substantial language here. Because *connecting* is something we read in an instant and understand deeper within us than language represents.

This elderly officer, it turned out, made an error in his call. It was he in the undercover car who first tracked the boys and called for backup. That error was forgivable, but it led to assumptive, aggressive behavior in the six who answered his call.

Who were all young.

In recent months, as I read article after article about civilians shot by police, I see bios of the officers that include a history of deployment in Iraq and Afghanistan. I have not gathered stats on this, I have simply read it, disturbingly, time and time again. A jaw-dropping statistic we do have, however, is that more veterans and active military have died by suicide than by combat in the past six years: 45,000. Do I want military officers to be employed after service? I do. They deserve job security upon their return from life-threatening work—and good health *and mental health* care. Do I want them in my backyard with guns? Well, they know how to use them, an argument perhaps in favor. But, well, they know how to use them in war.

It doesn't help that $7 billion worth of excess military stash has been gifted from the Pentagon to 8,000 law enforcement agencies nationwide—hand-me-downs of office equipment, clothing, tools, radios. *And* armored trucks, assault rifles, grenades and Mine-Resistant Ambush Protected vehicles. Priced at $800,000 per vehicle, *free* is quite the deal. But dress in combat gear and hop in that armored vehicle and look at the invitation to play soldier in suburban Maryland.

My backyard is where my cat Ginger is buried. It's where we had a little Bar Mitzvah brunch for one son, and a spring fair/birthday party for another—with the whole, globally-represented neighborhood tossing wet sponges at grown-ups, bobbing for marshmallows, and chugging homemade lemonade. It's where I've hidden plastic Easter eggs filled with jellybeans. It's where I like to practice yoga, in the gazebo we built.

Do I want a SWAT team to enter it?

Had they announced their presence we'd have invited them for barbecued chicken sandwiches and hot chocolate.

But they were in warrior mindset. And there was no reaching them.

If one can stomach watching the video of a white cop's knee on George Floyd's brown neck for eight minutes and forty-six seconds that will kill him, one knows that this Minnesota cop is racist, mentally sick, numbingly traumatized, former military, or all of the above. For eight years he was a Military Police Soldier with the Army Reserves. What he demonstrated was unmitigated aggression on an unarmed, handcuffed man; what he orchestrated was conscious reactive killing in a circumstance where he himself was in no danger. Like my main abuser, he had time to think after his first violent impulse, *but had no reflection*. His knee remains *on a neck*. "He was just looking around, not a care in the world," commented a former police commissioner, and we know that this nonchalant posture is the most frightening of all, for it means the man's nervous system is misfiring—there is an absence of human connectivity. His continuous perpetration of harm was sadistic and without sane boundary, as have been so many seen and unseen violations, the raw truth of which has rocked our country.

Now I fear for the handsome neighbor my sons grew up with, serving on the DC police force, a young man of sound mind and judgment. Not a traumatized person—he simply fulfilled his secret dream to become a cop, and he is exactly the police officer I would want to call for help. He is white but would condemn white supremacists. What danger has he just stepped into? What influences? Anger cycles and recycles; the fear in one set of eyes spreads fear to the next; the mental health status of our gun-wielding American citizens can be as questionable as the mental health and reactivity of our cops. Soon we're carrying guns to sleep. And to school. Don't get me started—this is supposed to be about therapists, and why I didn't see one.

The only path I knew was to tap creativity and regain power through meaningful action.

I testified for police reform in our state capital with the American Civil Liberties Union (ACLU) in a senate room terrifyingly jammed with blue-uniformed police chiefs. My husband joined me on the podium the second time, and several years later he initiated the first Policing Advisory Commission in our county, with representatives from the NAACP, Casa de Maryland, and local citizens. Defeat was frequent, progress deadly slow—the ACLU seemed used to this. I wrote books, articles, poems, prayed for strength.

And I turned to my practices, becoming—as I've trained myself over the years though never in the domain of police violence—my own how-to-recover-from-police-assault yoga therapist. That experience is chronicled in Appendix II of this book, the basis of all the acute trauma trainings I now offer—*to therapists.*

But note: These trainings do not revolve around relaxation techniques. They are strength-focused, vigilant, powerful. Because the honor we owe to the high alert system of a police assault victim, and any assault victim, is to meet that system with respect. After George Floyd's murder, a five-paged poem roared out of me, in part about the pseudo-therapy push to *heal*, when really, it's time to *act:*

> ...*resilience*
> is a four-letter construct to me. *Healing*
> is an insult. *Recovery*
> is an *ass* who doesn't get it...

Therapy arrives in the most unexpected places. Years ago I learned this when I went to the shoemaker. He is an elfin man in an old storefront near my home. When you enter, you hear him at work in the back room, hammering and manipulating leather, until he breaks from his work, always reluctantly, to come to the front counter. I was in a panic when I arrived there one day— new jazz shoes I'd just received for my big performance the next day had heels a different height than my old ones, and this was affecting my turns.

Not only did he shave down the heel right then and there, but when he handed them to me (the yoga therapist), he (the shoe repair man) looked deep in my eyes: *"Breathe!"* he said. "All you have to do is breathe."

Nor did I expect it would be therapeutic when the Investigative Sergeant and his deputy arrived to interview me at my house. It had taken three weeks of constant work to write up an official complaint to the Internal Affairs Bureau. I shook violently during the drive to Gaithersburg to deliver it. When Sergeant Schiff received it from me, it helped that he was not in uniform. Starched white shirt with slacks and a friendly face—such a surprise.

He scanned my complaint as I stood there. I wanted to leave. Alone in the office waiting room with him, I hadn't bargained to hang out while an officer looked at my accusations. On the form, there'd been official instructions to have the complaint stamped by a Notary Public *if* the event involved inappropriate force from the police.

"You'll have to get this notarized," Sergeant Schiff said.

"But it says..." I muttered. I had merely written up what happened. I had no name for it.

And I had no one on my side substantiating what I had experienced.

"This is police brutality," he said.

"Oh," I said.

I was quieted. I was volcanic inside. My words were being understood by a professional. I was being *seen* by someone who mattered, not by a psychotherapist who could help me with my *problem*, but with a law enforcement professional who understood the cause of my suffering.

"I knew that," I said, "but I didn't know you would know that."

I drove west a bit to find a notary public. I found one at a bank in a mall. The notary looked at my pages, looked up at me for a moment, and stamped my document.

Although it would be eight months before a determination would arrive from the Internal Affairs Division; and although that long-awaited letter would only hint that the police had been found at fault and "appropriate measures" taken; and although learning this surfaced in me new fears of retaliation from the faulted cops; the contact with Sergeant Schiff was both therapeutic and impactful.

Within a month after filing the complaint, three months after the assault, Sergeant Schiff and his assistant visited me at my home. I walked him through everything I remembered. We walked the length of my yard, I mimicked each point of conflict in the alley. They interviewed me for nearly two hours. Afterward, I felt listened to for the first time, and wrote him so in an email:

January 23, 2015
Sergeant Schiff,

Thank you for your thorough investigation this afternoon.
Of course, I later remembered things to add, but no matter.
I very much appreciated your time, your questions, and
the attitude with which you and Sergeant Teal conducted
the interview. I know it will help me restore faith.

He replied that it was helpful to get my feedback, and
important for the Division to remember this aspect of their job.
"Sometimes the best medicine can be telling others about your
ordeal," he wrote. That night I cooked dinner for my family for the
first time in eleven weeks.

INTERMEZZO 4

Missing Advocates and an APO

AUNT BERTHA SAID, *EAT DESSERT FIRST.* Her philosophy was based on several truths: One, you could die after dinner and totally miss dessert. Two, you could be too full after the main meal and be forced to pass on the best part. Three, you could run out of time. And four, you could surpass your dinner budget. The last two reflect Bertha's Londoner persuasion of dinner out followed by a show in Piccadilly Circus. Invariably it would be show time and she hadn't had her "sweet" yet, either running out of cash or—since her financial situation was legend and she was usually treated to dinner and a show—running short of time before curtain. Therefore, instructed Bertha, abolish the usual order of events and first eat the treat.

Bertha was really my husband's aunt, but you couldn't know Bertha and not have her for your own. In fact, she owned me before Robin and I officially married, linking arms with me as if claiming the moon as hers once she found out my political background. For I was to meet her while surrounded by the selectively deaf ears of her many opinionated siblings, Bertha being one of thirteen that included my husband's father. In London, I met most of them, save the two who died at birth (there were fifteen originally) and several others who'd passed on.

It was a tall order to meet this cerebral and grouchy group all in one room, exposing myself to their interviews, the youngest aged eighty. Invariably, the question arose, in repeated exchanges with one elder after another, each with his or her own motive for asking: *What does your father do?* I turned to Robin for assistance not only because I'd been forewarned about their varied political views and acerbic tongues, but because my father had held so many jobs I wasn't sure how to describe what he did. He was, I knew, a "good guy." He would pass away, to my great sadness, only a few years later, still in his fifties, and at the memorial service hundreds would gather. And those who couldn't attend due to distance—Coretta Scott King, Ted Kennedy, Morton Sobel, Bill Bradley—sent condolences by telegram. My father had been Bradley's first mayoral campaign manager in Los Angeles until, smeared by Sam Yorty as a Pinko, my father quickly resigned to protect the survival of the campaign.

It was my future husband's job to chime in with each aunt and uncle's interrogation regarding my father's occupation. To Lulu, he said, "He's a consultant." To Weenie, he said, "He's the Education Director of Cooperative Stores in California." To Tiny he said, "He's self-employed." To Michael and Betty he said, "He works as a mediator." And to Bertha, dear Bertha, he whispered too loudly for my taste, "He's a Communist." Although this wasn't accurate, it was true that my father was blacklisted during the McCarthy era, being a devoted activist for human rights of every kind, and I'd grown up fearing the FBI's knock.

Exposed nakedly like this in front of Bertha, I cringed to hear my father summarized this way, especially in surroundings where I was a stranger, not my country, not my relatives. Such insensitivity was a vote to cast against marrying this fellow—after all, how could he speak in ways that endangered my privacy and safety? My American friends and I had learned at a young age to turn on the radio when talking like this. Decades later, through the Freedom of Information Act, we would acquire my father's FBI files from the Library of Congress and find out that even his outside garbage cans had been rustled through, photographed and documented—a hidden gift half a century later when we saw microfilm files with postcards my grandfather wrote. But Robin had been spared such fears, and I didn't yet realize that he was calibrating exactly to whom he spoke in each coupling of conversation, smartly adjusting my father's livelihood.

"Welcome to the family!" toasted Bertha, with a handshake so hearty it shamed me given her tiny, scoliotic frame supported by a cane. From that moment on I was in Bertha's great favor, for she had devoted her life, as had my father, to protecting the underserved, and had emerged with this strength amid siblings who were not only many, but politically factioned against her.

Why am I writing to you about great Aunt Bertha, former reporter in Cairo and Budapest, and a diehard Londoner? For only one slightly sidetracked reason: because we have almost arrived at the last cellmate, a short chapter that both frightens me to write, and brings me to weeping, for it is about Mudd, who remains so poignant in the back of my eyes that my throat grabs to write her name. The top of my skull tenses like a drink shaken to explode, and I hold my cheeks and chin steady with one cupped hand as I write, willing the tears back in the library one day, in a coffee shop another day, and at my kitchen table yet another, where finally the dam holding my heart altogether breaks.

No, we were not lovers. We knew each other only as I knew my other cellmates, for select hours of the forever that is one night. But we connected in ways so horribly profound both in the cell and in the plot twist I was to find out days later, that I tremble to understand all that was Mudd.

Thus, writing about Mudd makes me think of Bertha. For I often follow Bertha's credo of "dessert first," and in these chapters I'm committing a digression from that right order of things. I have saved for you, and for me, the scant, potent dessert of what Mudd teaches us for last.

And one more reason for this off-topic harboring: there have been certain people I have missed to a stabbing degree throughout this ordeal, people who I believe would have been tireless in both their emotional support and in their action.

Too little of that combination was to be found. There was the ACLU of Maryland with their dogged legislative fight in our state capital. There was local activist Darian Unger, who listened, and guided us. And there were a few key people who invested in supporting me emotionally—my husband Robin who fed me and became number one parent, my co-counseling buddy Betty who held me while I shook and raged, and Academic Director Mary Partlow who said, "Then just write!" and waived my graduate school assignments for three months. Two of my siblings constantly checked in, my neighbor Carol was a savior when I called for help, cousin Jane counseled, "Stay with the allies," and Lyn, the Welsh dog-walking man, told me to hold on, hold on—to sanity, to marriage, to faith.

Every smile or sign of care in the two years following the assault remains imprinted in my mind: each face, where each person was, standing or in their car as they stopped; each kind word, no matter how awkward. I was desperate. A nod could get me by.

But were they alive, I have no doubt that it would have been my aunt-in-law, Bertha, and my father, Don, who would have embodied both the worldly activism and the unqualified personal advocacy I longed for—because they understood politics, the system, and power, and because Bertha and Dad would have required no proof to believe me.

And this point is not only a reflection on the white, middle-class ears who could not take in my story, but on the West Baltimore neighbors of Kali, another mother whose story paralleled mine: arrested while going to her son.

Yes, she verified: *Even some close friends and relatives didn't believe me.*

Where along the path of intelligent citizenry do we bend our humanitarian standards of the police and blame the victim? Faulting the victim, I would find out later, is a common mentality in scenarios of abuse and assault. So is the pattern of faulting oneself.

When I approached my ethics instructor at Maryland University of Integrative Health, to prep her that I'd been assaulted that week and might have attention limitations during lectures, I slipped in the words "probably something I did wrong," as I summarized the incident.

"Don't do that!" she exclaimed. A former practicing attorney, cancer-survivor, licensed acupuncturist, clinic director at MUIH, and openly gay, she'd been around the block. This was apparent by the pain on her face and the instant comprehension of my story. Like an umpire calling a strike at a tense pitching moment, she called *"trap!"* Clearly, she wanted to grab my shoulders, drive sense into my marrow through her own fingers of knowledge and strength. Perhaps she had experience with assault and knew the patterns of self-blame: *"Don't do that—don't do that—don't do that,"* she begged.

It's a twist of modern times that Kali in West Baltimore, and I in Montgomery County, both experienced the similar judgment: *You should have known better.* It reflects back to politicians, and beyond the politicians to one's relatives, friends, neighbors, who squint their eyes like you're Borat at the dinner table, clueless of the protocol in a First World country: You poop in the toilet, leave it there, and flush—doesn't everyone know that? Similarly, *no matter what the police do or say, you stand still.*

Apparently, everyone knows this, this distillation of information that implies a certain uncivilized nature in the police, unreachable by normal means of communication (such as speaking, explaining), even if it provides them with essential facts. *You stand still, you hold still, you don't speak.* Kali's son was being beaten by the police, and she—who testified next to me on a panel in Annapolis at the State House of Representatives—crossed the street and went to him, only to find herself handcuffed and pushed to the curb. "Like an animal," she told me. To Kali, who watched her son's pants pulled down as he was beaten, the highest insult of all was when she was forced to sit on a dirty curb, handcuffed and helpless to her son.

When did the memo go out that we moms missed, the one that says, *Don't move, don't speak, don't go to your son when any gang—government-paid or otherwise—is holding or hurting him?* And when that memo did go out, did it include some prophylactic to block the hormonal cocktail that gives a mom superhuman faculties as protector of the soul she birthed, nursed, and caught with one hand when he fell from the slide, protector of the child whose key in the door she waits to hear every night since he turned teen? If we shame the passionate drive to go to another in need, don't we disclaim the best of our mammalian biology? Rather than a self-defense course, do we now need to take a course called *learning how to suck it up when the police are beating someone you love?*

Yes, in fact Kali now helps the ACLU in offering "Know Your Rights" seminars. I attended one and started shaking and sobbing when they showed the "Know Your Rights" teaching film of aggressive police (portrayed by actors) assaulting innocent citizens (also actors) and the how-to's and how-not-to's of the citizens' response.

I had been a how-not-to.

I spent the first six months after this assault re-playing the event. Middle of the day, middle of the night, my mind ran daydreams and nightmares, testing scenarios where I or the police made a different choice. Even in the most idyllic fantasy version in which I had just been meditating and was "centered" as I entered the backyard to see why seven police had broken in and taken my teens, the fact that I still faced shocking disrespect and aggression made for an unchanging outcome: my face in the dirt, the threat of tasing, the forcing into handcuffs.

The reason for this was that I could not undo the fact of being a mom, even in the setting of fantasy retakes. I could not eliminate the part of walking to my son. I could not *not* walk to my son.

Here's a variation I half-dreamed while unable to sleep one of many nights:

The police say I have to go back into my house (as they really did say). They aggressively bar me from exiting beyond my gate (as they really did) and shine a high-beam light directly in my eyes to intimidate me to retreat (as happened). They assert that I cannot bear witness while they question the boys (as occurred).

But in this scenario I cooperate. I let them back me away from this frightening alley scene, where kids I'm in charge of are surrounded in the dark by heavily armed men and women who are behaving like bullies rather than protectors of the law. I let them back me away. Against all my chemistry I walk the three steps backwards through my gate.

But then I high-tail it to the gazebo, grab a chair, and place it in the far corner of the yard, where I climb upon it and remain inside my fence, looking over to the immediate scene in the alley. I am legal according to their demand, but I am doing my duty as a parent and a responsible adult, watching to make sure my kids stay safe.

I am screaming next and it is my voice and it is real and my husband is woken and I cannot stop, though he holds me thank god to make the lancing to my heart bearable. For I have been defeated and I have been shot, multiple times.

I am riddled with bullets and do a horrible scarecrow dance in airborne spasms from atop my chair perch. Shrieks erupt with each gunshot to my body, and all this my younger son witnesses in horror, infinitely damaging him from the other side of the fence.

The result of these workings and re-workings of the event are that eventually I became satisfied. That no matter what I had done, I was up against a force with zero room for one super-simple fact relevant to, if no one else, me. I was a mom. And that trumped all the rest.

I was ill-educated on the sway of the Fraternal Order of Police, ill-equipped to speak in police dialect, and the extent of APO— Assault on a Police Office—arrests in D.C. had not yet hit the press, but did on May 9, 2015 with the article, "Assault on Justice." When I heard Kojo Nnamdi's interview with investigative reporter Patrick Madden on our local NPR station as I was driving home from school, I had to pull to the side of the road, my vision so blinded by tears. Because there were a million versions of my story, and this trap had a name.

———

ASSAULT ON JUSTICE

BY PATRICK MADDEN, CHRISTINA DAVIDSON
Saturday, May 9th, 2015

Wiggling while handcuffed. Bracing one hand on the steering wheel during the arrest. Yelling at an officer.

All these actions have led to people being prosecuted for "assaulting a police officer" in Washington, D.C., where the offense is defined as including not just physical assault but also "resisting, opposing, impeding, intimidating or interfering" with law enforcement.

A five-month investigation by WAMU 88.5 News and the Investigative Reporting Workshop at American University, co-produced by Reveal, documented and analyzed nearly 2,000 cases with charges of assaulting a police officer. The results raise concerns about the use or overuse of the charge. Some defense attorneys see troubling indicators in these numbers, alleging that the law is being used as a tactic to cover up police abuse and civil-rights violations.

As protests and rioting have exploded across the country in response to police conduct, even Cathy Lanier, the chief of police in the nation's capital, is urging lawmakers to revise the statute because its broad application "naturally causes tensions between police and residents."

———————————

The police could move, but I could not move. They could touch me, but I was not to touch them. They could yell at me, but I could not yell in pain. If they jumped me and tried to handcuff me, (even without mentioning that I was under arrest), to "resist" for any reason—including confusion as to what was going on, or the fact that I'd painstakingly healed both arms from rotator cuff injuries and they were ripping my arms behind me—was a crime.

I'd been raised by a pacifist father who didn't allow us to point even dish soap at each other in pretense of shooting. And I was over-educated in my empathic training of stress-reduction for law enforcement, an unfortunate knowledge base at this instant, as it meant I assumed we could communicate. In graduate school, when a Chief of Police from Virginia arrived in full gear to our classroom, she and her Sergeant Deputy spent three hours on a Friday night educating us on the need for stress reduction programs for law enforcement. The Sergeant Deputy spoke intimately about excruciating headaches, stomach problems, back pain and paralyzing depression she suffered from on the job trauma in a macho environment that prevented her from seeking help—until her despair became dangerous. Males within the male-dominated force have it worse, she said, adding that the brave cops who took the yoga series my professor offered their department said it helped—even while wearing full gear in *savasana*. We dropped the police/civilian divide despite their loaded holsters and ended by chanting *OM* followed by hugs. I wrote the thank you card for my cohort of twenty-four yoga therapists.

Silly, silly, dangerously silly me. The police in my yard were not thinking about "mindfulness-based practices." They were hyper-activated. My status as mother, homeowner, good citizen, mattered not at all. Had I added that I was a Yoga Therapist it would have been another bad Borat joke.

In Emergency Response Training the first thing we learned was *Scene Assessment*. But the police didn't assess that they'd entered a family scene unannounced and taken kids from a barbecue. In whose backyard did they think their actions would *not* create a fear response?

But wait. What exactly did happen? Right before they jumped me, what sparked them into action? What made the main bully cop shout "That's assault!" prompting me to wonder in the nanosecond before they jumped on my back, who they were referring to.

I mentally rewind and rehash the conversation. I search for what happened just prior to that moment. I see my son in the distance with cops around him. Forgive me if I repeat myself, but I must admit something.

"That's my son!" I say.

"You can't talk with him," the blonde female cop says.

"Then I won't talk, I'll stand near him," I say.

She does not respond, there is a pause, and I understand that to mean we've reached a compromise.

I walk down the alley toward my son.

Why is the blonde cop here again? My replay of this doesn't make sense, but it is what I recall.

She blocks my way, stands in a power stance in front of me, Jolly Green Giant style.

"I am just walking to my son," I say.

And what happens now?

Does she angle her body so I cannot pass?

Does her body touch me, does she smack me with an elbow, or just intimidate, the way you can cross your arms and arm-butt to dissuade passage?

Does she lay her hands on my arms? Yes, I believe that is what she does.

Do I shrug her off, slipping out to continue walking past her? Yes, I recall this is what I do.

But do I touch her arm with my palms?

Do I push her when I shrug her off, or push past her so I can keep going? Or do I just shrug free?

This is the muddy part I do not entirely trust.

This is the part I don't write until nearly three years later, when I no longer feel guilty for any version of the above. A force was in the way of me getting to my son. I didn't know that I had to defer to it. And I'm not sure I'd have cared if I'd known. She might have put her hands on my upper arms. I might have shrugged them off. In the process, my body might have contacted hers.

"That's ASSAULT!" were the next words I heard. The sound was male, declarative and accusative, reminiscent of the words *Caught! Caught! Caught!* when we'd grab the flag-bearer in Capture the Flag at my grandparents' summer camp, tingling with excitement, the captured party tingling with fear. Regardless of whether the blonde cop had grabbed me, whether I'd slithered my arms away, or I'd in some form touched her, from his distant view in the dark, the bully cop saw APO.

Two men were on my back then. I had no idea why.

I continued walking to my son, the bully cop hanging on my right, the skinnier male cop on my left. It is at this moment that you hear my voice on the video, channeling my dad:

"For crying out loud, I'm just walking to my son!"

I am still thinking that we can iron this out.

I am kicked to the ground in a most technically admirable way. For it is smooth, and recalls the time I went with my older son, Daniel, to observe the wrestling class he had to take in middle school P.E., where the 300-pound coach barked "Attack!" and each boy knocked his partner's legs out from under him with a quick sweep, or a crazy-simple forced bend to the back of the knees.

The impact upon landing to my knees was jolting. It surprised me to suddenly go from the mission of walking, to the begging posture of kneeling.

I was pushed to my face while my arms were pulled behind me. I heard, "That's 'resisting arrest'!" which I only now know to place in quotes. At the time, I did not get it that I was in double trouble: that these were not *just* a cop's threatening words, they were criminal charges.

His partner successfully folded my left arm behind me like a broken wing. My right was the more sensitive of the two, with injury upon injury making me so protective of it, wanting to still dance, wanting to still swan-lake my arms, or jazz-hands them.

The rest I have told you: My walrus roar, "You're HURTING me!" because the bully cop was twisting and pulling my delicate right arm out of the socket. Are you wondering how I could not know he was trying to handcuff me? This truth I can guarantee: It did not occur to me.

I have never watched a cop show. I do not go to scary movies. My kids joke that I had conniptions during the animated *Monsters, Inc.*, and grabbed their thighs in fear.

One exception: Our dad allowed us (then four siblings and me) to watch *The Man from U.N.C.L.E.* perhaps once or twice. We're talking circa 1964. That was because the star, Robert Vaughn, had been the celebrity seated high in a red convertible, slow-waving as it floated at 2 mph alongside us civil rights marchers in Cleveland when I was nine. My father had organized that peace march. He'd agreed that we could now watch this "good guy" on TV. My father had no idea that *The Man from U.N.C.L.E.* was about secret agents with guns, and once he found out, that was the end of watching Robert Vaughn, who by the way, was shockingly short.

I did not know the game of cops and robbers.

Perhaps my son saved my life at that moment. He certainly saved my future by daring to videotape, against the orders of the cop who stood guard next to him.

The cop wrenching my right arm shouted the words I have already written: "Stop resisting or I'm going to have to tase you!"

The meaning of these words was taking too long to filter into my brain.

I had to decipher "tase."

I had to decipher "stop resisting."

I understood that he was referring to me, but did not understand that I was "resisting" him, in the formal accusation of the word, only that I was resisting having been pounced on and having my rotator cuffs torn by attackers.

I am not stupid.

But, like Gerald McBoing Boing and Amelia Bedelia, I have a certain slowness with language. My focus was singular: Get to Mikey; get these jerks off my back to get to Mikey.

"Mom. Mom! You've got to do it!"

This language had fragrance to it.

It entered my mind.

The words, the tone, the love of my son, the concern in his voice, the wisdom, all permeated and made sense.

Voice and tone and cadence, and language choice, make a great difference to the receptors of my brain, of *the* brain. *This* is ventral vagal communication. I received his information. I rescinded power.

Bertha and my dad would not have doubted my choices. They would not have had to do the physics re Scene Assessment, or comprehend Mama Bear Syndrome, or debrief on The Neuroscience of Oral Communication Between Humans. They would have simply endorsed me, believed me, and they would have needed no proof. Though there are many people who love me, few understood the extent of the transgression that occurred. To face peoples' doubt of the validity of this ordeal—as happens commonly after sexual assault, police assault, domestic assault—added enormously to the suffering and *moral injury*, a term coined by trauma scholar Jonathan Shay: "a betrayal of what's right by someone who holds power."

The moral injury would persist to this day. It requires deep, endlessly deeper, deeper than a keyboard can evoke, digging to the bottom-line truth under the muck. It requires warding off the tide of overwhelming shoulda-couldas that persist and riled my ethics instructor who heard the machinations of my mind: *You should have known better. You should have stood still.*

No. *They* should have known better. For he was my son, he is my job, he is my creation, he is my body, he is my duty, he is my light, he is the magnet calling me to move and protect and so I do move.

My father and Bertha would have risen to their feet and done *what* I don't know, but something different than the nothing that happened around me in response. Something very wrong happened in our backyard. It was emblematic of something very wrong happening in our society. And our society had gained ground only to the point of two things:

1) Adjusting *to* dangerous police behavior by training citizens to stand still even if watching a loved one brutalized; and

2) Explaining police aggression as a reflection of racial prejudice and minority profiling, an obvious truth, but an incomplete one.

I had found out firsthand that there was a sickness in our law enforcement that was additional to and overlapped with the sickness of racism. Six of seven police men and women in my backyard had no stopping mechanism, only a hair-raising escalation track, and once looped into it, the trapped individual was most likely to come out dead or damaged.

Our County Executive—then Ike Leggett, who is Black—when asked in a fiscal meeting to budget for police body cameras and de-escalation training, responded with, "What's 'de-escalation training'?" as if we were talking Greek. His reply to my personal story was that the police who assaulted me were "a few bad apples," a phrase also used by the Boston Diocese, until the Boston Globe reporters revealed more than 160 Catholic priests in Boston alone had molested 815 kids—and that was just the number of formal complaints. Of course there are wonderful priests; of course there are devoted cops—kind, skilled, and heroic ones too—but the apples metaphor is also an avoidance tactic so we won't scope out the system in which they grow, and we'd be wise to check where it landed the Catholic church: a little rotten fruit revealed a nation's orchard infestation. In fact, a global crisis.

Inflict the least harm possible to reach a beneficial outcome, is the basic code of non-maleficence in bioethics. Instead, our county's top brass protected the cops who dealt their handy APO card, a maleficent move that framed me as a criminal and let them off. *I* assaulted four police officers, and *I* resisted arrest.

As The Social Worker read my charges out loud, her clear voice reverberating in the hollow cell, our mates kept respectfully mum. Only Richmond focused gently on us with interest—the others cast their eyes elsewhere as if they were busy; busy doing nothing. Alexa closed her eyes. Mudd turned her head. I leaned on the cold cement wall. The Social Worker stood straight and tall; her words began to seep in...*I was at fault*...those trusty sister themes Blame and Shame I'd meet so often in later years listening to clients. Blame would come at me via citizens as well as cops, as in the email commentary, if not the silence, of certain friends and relatives. "But I've always had good rapport with the police," emailed one white neighbor, which prompted me to stare at the screen and go numb.

But now I must tell you about Mudd. And a sad plot-twist of dessert it is, too. I look up from the keyboard and ask the cement building in the distance if Mudd survived her demise and the multi-layered trap she fell into, a trap that portrays our culture's incessant cycle of racism-fueled oppression, poverty, and incarceration. The building answers back with the unknown, expressed in the sadness of its taupe and grey walls. We will never know what happened to Mudd and her children. But we can tell her story.

For this is the gift she gave me in the cell, and that which we can give each other at every harsh juncture: the gift of connecting even if only with a few words, and eyes that say, *I see.*

CHAPTER 5

Mudd

———

*"The men who shot him didn't see *him*," I finally said, my voice unsteady. "He asked for help, but all they saw was an image based on how he looked... I don't want to be like that with anyone."*

I took a deep breath.

"I want people to know that I see them..."

—DONNA BRITT, "BROTHERS (& ME)"

MUDD

MUDD WAS THE NAME *I came to know best because she always had her arms down her sweatpants—all the way in her pant legs as if she was doing a version of that parlor skit we did at camp, one person's arms hidden behind so they are armless while the second person performs the gestures to her story. Except that no one gestured for Mudd's story. It was only an armless Mudd, so cold as to double over with her arms warmed by her own silk thighs. "Take your arms out of your pants, Mudd!" I heard the guard say repeatedly, so I learned her name with every clang of keys.*

It was Mudd's kindness that recorded like an engraving in my heart and in my vision, so that I see her exactly as she was, armless and looking as desperately to me for help as I looked to her. So that even now as I look out the Starbuck's window to the pedestrian scene of umbrellas and black coats, all I see while I stare at DSW Shoes' display plastered across the street is Mudd. Everything about her is neutral as if someone had suggested a pallet of neutral tones to blend with the cell environment— grey sweat pants, beige T shirt with capped sleeves, a soft grey-brown face, her neck and upper biceps the only parts not inverted into her billowing legs.

I had used the bathroom. It took three hours of tortured holding in until I finally organized the women so I could use the toilet. The bathroom was part of the cell, with just a concrete, hip-height wall to imply discretion. Any sound or odor was as shared as one's presence on the toilet in the cell. "Could I ask a favor of all of you?" I finally blurted out, and then proceeded rapidly into my topic so as not to leave them dangling on the word "favor"—scratch her back? Help her escape? Change the words on her charges papers? The fantasies could go too far even with this normal, everyday phrasing—Can you do me a favor?— compromised as we were by fear, sleep-deprivation, dazing lights, and the blaring TV in the upper corner, the last combative force that broke up any chance of forming coherent thought.

"Could you all possibly move toward that corner so I could have some privacy in the bathroom?"

My desperation was now 200 percent. There was no more question of self-respect or modesty. That, too, had been replaced in a remarkably short time, by the pure animal need to relieve myself. It was that or— drama aside—die. Hours earlier I'd been tackled and shackled by a SWAT team-like group of seven armed police, toll enough on bladder and bowel. But now, time ticked on in that discouraging way, that hopeless way, because we knew that the youngest in our group, Baby, who had just been called out to see The Commissioner, had been waiting not four hours as I had done so far, but sixteen, and they were by law permitted to hold me here for seventy-two. There was still no sign of food or drink or a blanket for sleep.

My cellmates were happy to move to one corner. This was now a grouped cluster of women who were no more common to each other than if you randomly plucked any four humans from the street. Yet they clustered for me along a far edge of the cell like old friends. They themselves had resisted that toilet for the duration, but then they had mostly been handcuffed in their homes, not jumped by the police.

I was quick in the bathroom. And the women knew to talk loudly amongst themselves for my privacy. It was later, much later, when I was chatting with Mudd about the surveillance camera I recalled seeing earlier in the hall, that I realized exactly where in our cell the video camera seemed to point.

"Oh, my God. It picks up the toilet area!"

"No, I don't think so," said Mudd.

"Do you think it's projected on one of their screens in the hall where all the guards can see?"

"No. Look at the angle. I don't think it can pick up the toilet area," said Mudd.

There was a long pause then. Or maybe it was not at all long. But in my heart it is a beat-stopper. And even now, staring out the Starbucks window watching two boys, one dressed all in purple sipping from a shiny red water bottle, all I feel and see is the stoppage of time. It is connection and intimacy: Mudd's eyes across the cell from mine.

We are looking at each other. Like two friends ching/ching/chinging a recognition of each other after thirty years, or like two cats frozen before a fight. It is only Mudd's eyes and my eyes. Are hers beseeching? Why would her eyes beseech me?

The pause is a stillness and the disappearance of everyone else in the cell and outside the cell. The sound of the TV racket is no noise to me now. I am locked in the story in Mudd's eyes.

"Are you... Are you just being kind?" I ask. For it has dawned on me that she might be lying to help me cope. My mother's style of a lie.

Mudd doesn't answer, but her eyes don't leave mine either. As if assigned that exercise of sitting across from a stranger and gazing into each other's eyes for four minutes; it is an eternity of grace and discomfort. Just her lips do that expression thing we do with the slightest inflection in our shoulders, something that communicates a noncommittal Maybe or, Who Knows, neither a Yes or a No.

She is protecting me from knowledge. Her sad eyes are a sister's, withholding information to keep me from pain. We don't speak of it further. We pass.

MUDD HAD TOLD ME HER STORY. She has two children, ages three and eighteen months. She'd tried to break up with her boyfriend recently. They were always arguing and she didn't like the people he was hanging with, a younger brother, a cousin, and their friends.

"They like to beat up pedestrians and steal their cash and phones," said Mudd.

They what? She had said this casually, or she had said it with sadness, I don't know which. She spoke the words fast; maybe I didn't hear right.

"You mean they demand cell phones and beat people up if they don't give them," I said, suggesting a switch of her sentence parts.

"No. They beat people up and take their cell phones."

Oh my God, I thought. *Sammy*. My nephew had been living with us while he looked for a house share. He typically walked home from the Silver Spring metro after closing a restaurant in Georgetown, sometimes at 12:00 midnight, 12:30, or later. Sam is 5'8". And I'm Arnold Schwarzenegger if he's anything more than 140 pounds. I worried about him every night until I heard his key, and now I had even more reason to.

Thank goodness we live far from here, I thought to myself, imagining that Mudd and her boyfriend's crew lived close to this cell where the cops took me, way west of my house on the Beltway, and somewhere north, up-county a good distance.

Mudd and her boyfriend had been arguing day and night she said, and she wanted all the guys out of her house. Then she missed her period and two pregnancy tests showed positive. When she told him the news, her boyfriend became very tender and the next few days went smoothly. She decided to let him stay.

But when they hung with all the other guys, Mudd said, her boyfriend, his cousin, and friends would be walking along and suddenly decide to take down a pedestrian, beating him up and robbing him.

"What do you mean, 'beating him up'?" I asked. She spoke so mundanely, I wasn't confident that I'd matched up the words.

"Breaking his nose or something."

She continued: "I don't like it, and I always try to walk a different direction when they go after someone."

"Wait," I said. "You're walking along, and out of the blue, they branch off to follow someone?"

"Yeah, and I'll go the other way if I can. But sometimes they come back to my house afterward."

On this Hallowe'en night, they'd all been walking together, and the guys did it again, beating someone up and robbing them. Afterwards they went to Mudd's.

The police showed up at her house. They had a search warrant. A gun showed up in the search. Mudd was arrested. Her boyfriend, and his cousins or cousin and a friend were . . .

. . . writing this, I leave those words blank to *check with Mudd and fill them in later.*

What am I thinking? That I can text her? That we exchanged cell phone numbers? No paper, no pens, no phones. No earrings, no hair scrunchies, no bobby pins, no shoes, no jacket, no pocket with a wrinkled sales receipt you could scratch a number on. Just our minds, and they were compromised. No one tried to exchange information by memory to "hey, just stay in touch."

"I don't know what to do," Mudd said, in a monotone that matched everything else bland about her; even her eyes were dulled, all expression safely hidden except a vulnerable goodness you could divine beneath. She'd come out of her corner just a little way—funny how a body chooses a spot, even in jail. Walk into a yoga studio and take someone's favorite spot near the wall and you'll feel deadly eyes bore through you when they register the offense of their safe wall taken. Same at a ballet barre, or even one's place at a dinner table, or a study space, library, or bus. When I see each of my cellmates in my mind's eye, I see them physically in the spot or spots they gravitated to that night, as if they belonged right in those few inches. For Mudd it was that far right corner. I see her. Her arms are down her grey sweatpants with her back to the corner so she can see all aspects of the cell, exactly how I sat in bed, nights after my mother died if my father was out late. I waited and watched, the corner had my back and I was vigilant: seeing the door mattered.

When I say Mudd's hands were down her pants, I mean she'd inverted her body like a diver into water, as deep into her stretchy sweats as she could dive, her torso immersed in a sea of grey, her arms disappeared and therefore her body crouched in two. But her neck had to arch up because, as anyone who's been through a trauma knows, you better keep your eyes on the lookout. It was a brilliant forward bend and it was cold enough in that cell that I'm sure she'd have come out the ankle end, hands through her elastic cuffs, if she could. She spoke to me from there, an eye-opening, continuous stream of thought; Mudd was a profound silence hunched over, but when she spoke, her unexpressive delivery went right in. If I knew there were past lives, I'd have said she was my soulmate or sister before, because her words simultaneously hurt to the core and melted my freezing chest.

"If I go to jail, I won't see my kids till they're ten and my dad would never bring them to see me and when I come out I'll have a felony like my brother who is such a good worker that Giant wanted to hire him but he can't get any job cause of his felony charges. If I take the plea bargain and tell on my boyfriend's cousin"—who led the spontaneous beating up and robbing of tonight's pedestrians—"his crew would probably hurt me and my children . . . I guess I could go to my Mom in Florida but her boyfriend doesn't like kids."

Much later, when The Commissioner allowed me to be unhandcuffed from his desk and return briefly to my cell to make a phone call—a desperate event when the phone repeatedly cut me off every time I managed to get a ring tone—it was Mudd who came to my rescue. The Commissioner by then was probably shitting his own bricks that this sixty-year-old Montgomery County homeowner with a pristine record had been assaulted and carted here by the police, and so he had agreed to hold my place in the line-up while I consulted with my husband on whether to use a public defender or tell my story myself. I had one shot at getting this right, and after being awake for twenty-two hours, I could barely see through my contact lenses, much less stand on my feet to orchestrate another call.

Every time I had to redial the 1 and the 1 and the 3 and the 3 according to the recorded instructions, I would be cut off, only to start again. I had trouble because I was trembling so much.

I have benign tremors—tonight they were raging. Rushing to make this call quickly, while in the middle of the long-awaited investigation with The Commissioner where I'd sat surrounded by armed guards talking through the dots in a bulletproof window, I was shaking to a theatrical degree.

The squares of numbers on this bizarre phone were large enough. Anyone could press these. They were larger than the keys on my keyboard. But even steadying one trembling hand with another, I kept miss-pressing, sending me back to the beginning like a Chutes and Ladders game, every step so painstaking, with my ear pressed hard to the ear hole (literally, a hole), with my mouth ready to jump down to the mouth hole to shout. Seeing my frustration, young, twenty-something Mudd came over to me.

"Do you want me to help you?" she asked.

It's worth remembering we were both being held as criminals. It is worth noting this was my home phone number we were dialing. I paused for an uncomfortably long moment and looked at Mudd. I needed her. What's more, I trusted her.

"Yes. Please help," I said.

INTERMEZZO 5

Post-Assault
Prescription When I Fear My
Spirit Dying

To Coretta Scott King and Dr. Martin Luther King, Jr.;
and to my parents.

1st draft January 2015 / final draft October 2019

First Prize in Split This Rock's
2020 Sonia Sanchez-Langston Hughes Poetry Contest
Judged by Richard Blanco

Here in the mud
of my history
beneath the rage
is counsel.

Where grace
expands like the air
under a bird's wings
all day it seems,

rising
soaring
gliding.

Willingness
to take the air
and ride it
is grace.

Riding,
being lifted
by air
is grace.

I seek grace now
as my rage deepens
exponentially
to hate.

As I see my own dreams –
the day ones
the night –

and witness my capacity
to do to another
real harm.

I return to silence
I am not saying
it is easy.

I return to silence
I am not saying
I will be quiet.

I return to silence
I am not saying
I won't shout my grief
from the rooftops.

I am saying
Silence, old friend,

take me to wings
for the moment

lend me levity

remind my breath
of breath
beneath breath

and the untapped wisdom
beneath that.

Take me to updrafts
or wind loops
my father soared

that lifted my mother
when her grief
took hold.

They have been this path
these kings
these queens.

They have dug
to the deepest
of rage

to the place
where the body
is a volcano of anger

where hate is so tempting
it begins to
taste great

and you
start
to want it.

Silence.

(The heart is a
blanket that lies
soft to the spine

she whispers
to the pounding heels:
Now! Even now –

face rosen
with the swelling of
terror

stomach a gutter of
moral injury

hair torn
ragged from violation
in this backyard...)

Silence
is the heart's banner
in 200 mph fear.

She pulse-flashes
in sky-fire across
my lacerated faith.

She glares down
the clutch of despair
in my gullet

singing glorified lyric
over hammering percussion:

Find silence!
Garner power!

And sweat-soaked in prayer,
incredulous with doubt

hardly the soaring bird and
beg-kneeling
ancient in the muck I

hear her start this
odd duet of continuance:

tether-tether, she whispers,
heels to the molten then

Let.
Open.
Wings.

And I in my
mammal weight wonder

now?

Walking in the
bones of a distant girl?

Now?
Mad gravel between two lips?

Even now,
she answers mercilessly

as if it's simple.
As if it's known.

Even
now.

For an audio reading of this poem, please visit:

https://www.splitthisrock.org/images/uploads/
Diana_Tokaji_Post-Assault_Perscription_When_I_Fear_
My_Spirit_Dying_Audio.mp3

CHAPTER 6

Get Out of Jail
(Not) Free

———

When someone shows you who they are,
believe them the first time.

—MAYA ANGELOU

GET OUT OF JAIL (NOT) FREE

I AM LOCKED IN A small room. There are no windows—of course there are no windows; nowhere has there been a window. I am locked in succession by a wrought iron grated door that has banged behind me, then a solid metal door, shutting me into a 6'x6' space whose neutral walls are slippery concrete or painted metal. I do not explore them. Touching things is not an option.

My hands had followed a series of orders: up the hall wall for pat down, handcuffed behind me as I was led from the hall through the succession of locking doors, and now this: I am told to sit at a scratched-up metal table to which I am then physically locked. My left handcuff is clicked with the spin of a key into a tight iron ring on the metal desk. I'm not going anywhere unless I haul the table too.

We make an odd trio, me and the two guards who escorted me here. They lock me in place—every locking mechanism an intimidating click or clang or slam—then stand like sentinels to either side of my chair and slightly behind, so that I can't see them as I'm being questioned. But I can feel them. As a dancer or performer, you train to feel other performers on stage without turning your head. You notice if you're in sync with the unison movement, observe all subtle cues, only whispering to each other if your head momentarily faces away from the audience. Otherwise, your performance relies on that developed sense of peripheral vision and an animalistic way of feeling the air. Right now, I'm definitely feeling the air, and it's charged.

Overall, the guards maintain an attitude of disdain. They are in power / we do what they say. But as I sit shaking between their armed presences at what I later decide was about 3:00 a.m., I sense a shift in them from disdain to resentment. The ensuing interview reveals that beyond my current ragtag look, I lead a modest but nearly middle-class existence, with education, house, marriage, and some privileged associations. The air prickles around me; it gets heavy as I craft my answers.

"Address?" "Phone?" "Place of birth?" "Date of birth?" The Commissioner is the one white person I have seen among the prison staff. From the time the young white cop led me out of his speeding squad car until now, every pat down, every lock up, every escort, and now the two standing sentinels, has been a man or woman who is Black. With my first thumbprint came a guard's reference to "The Commissioner"— words that escaped my understanding as thoroughly as a pub order for "a Guinness" confounded me when I was an eighteen-year-old waitress in London and knew no beers (it sounded like an arrhythmic order for "Agnes"). "When you're called to The Commissioner..." was just another blur of language on a planet without normal conversation. But there was a tone as if getting there was the Emerald City at the end of the yellow brick road, potentially our key to freedom. What would my cellmates and I go through to get there? When would we be called, and, alone and already terrified, would we know what to say, how to act? Would we say it "right" so we could get out of jail? Real information came only inside the cell, when Baby, the youngest of us, said we can

be held in the cell a maximum of three days. "Until you're called to see *The Commissioner,*" she said clearly, those owl eyes looking straight into mine, and I got it. *The Wizard was our ticket out.*

Baby was the first one called. And then she was gone. Out of nowhere came a rattle of keys, a slam as the cell door banged open—yes, banged open—a name shouted by a voice with no face, and the cellmate who'd been summoned, walked out. Nothing to gather up—just a catch in that woman's throat, the quick contracting of her body toward the door, the disappearance of her heel, the slam, clang, resounding *hunnnngh,* and then the silence of her absence, weakening our hub and inciting a moment of pause as we registered that she was separated from us, alone.

Now, the all-powerful Commissioner, a bald-headed, sixty-something man, sits three feet away from me on the other side of two sheets of greying Plexiglas, his profile all I see. He asks me my name. He reads me my charges, and I am grateful to *The Social Worker* for reciting them to me first. He questions me in a monotone—no flinching, no expression, no eye-contact. *I fumble to make coherent answers to simple questions pertaining to my status. I fumble even more to summarize what happened with the police in my backyard. Fortunately, in a key advisory moment, Mudd had prepped me in rhetoric:*

"*Don't call them cops when you speak to The Commissioner,*" she'd told me several hours in advance, before I even understood that Oz was waiting. In conversation, she'd caught the drift of my angry word choices, and although I didn't know it then, was kindly saving my ass.

"*Call them officers when you speak to him,*" she said, and my look of incomprehension must have worried her, as I had no idea what was coming. But here, in sentinel-guarded, locked-to-the-table security, *with double panes of blur and bullet-proof between me and the man with the power to let me go home, I am 100 percent understanding Mudd's linguistic cue. My body is raging like I'd swallowed neon steroids, but you bet I remember to refer to the cops who'd just assaulted me as "officers."*

"How long have you lived at this address?"

"We've owned our home for twenty-five years," I say. There's stillness in the room.

"What's your highest monthly expense?"

"Ummm....college tuition?" Our older son was in his senior year of college; our younger son applying; and I was in graduate school.

"Where do you work?"

"Ummm...Strathmore Center for Music and the Performing Arts. In Bethesda," I add, keeping to myself that I also see clients in their homes in different parts of town—it just wouldn't have sounded right. "Strathmore" and "Bethesda," however, were words to include, they have ramifications in our county—that's the wealthy side of town. Upon hearing that I work there, I feel the pale Commissioner grow paler, sniffing the possibility of error on the part of the police, the possibility of a law suit from this woman propping her chin up with her not-handcuffed hand, shaking visibly, occasionally putting her head on the table, unable to breathe, gasping.

His fingers pause at the keyboard. I feel the clicking of his brain in the silence as my words sink in. He avoids turning his head to look at me, but I sense he wants to. His neck pivots ever so slightly in my direction. Is he thinking, this could be my wife? *The sentinels behind me have caught the entire play.*

"Any parking tickets?" he asks.

"No."

"Moving violations?"

"No."

"Any misdemeanors, felony charges, any..." he rattles off an extensive list of potential criminal activity I could not define if I was asked, but the answer, I'm clear, is "No."

"Do you have a lawyer?"

"No. I've never needed a lawyer."

The Commissioner recites my lawyer choices, telling me that before I report my version of what happened, he's required to tell me my legal options. I can wait an unknown amount of time to be assigned a public defender, I can hire my own lawyer to advise me, or I can simply report my story now. The first two options require delay in my release. It is the middle of the night; tomorrow is Saturday. But he has recited my options so fast and my brain is so compromised as well as ignorant in legalese that I am panicking while trying to decide what to choose. Is there a hidden risk if I report what happened without a lawyer present? Is a public defender (free or low cost) less capable or less motivated *or less on my side than a hired (expensive) lawyer? If I speak without protection of a lawyer, will my husband say that was the worst thing to have done, that I shouldn't have panicked and caved? If only I could consult him, if only The Commissioner could advise me, if only one of these sentinels could speak, since everyone here knows the safest choice that will let me out and protect my future.*

"Is there a phone I could use? Could I call my husband?" This seems like a far-fetched hope.

The Commissioner thinks for a minute. I'm sweating. I know I'm old enough to make my own decisions and I should know my rights and my legal moves. But instead, I know the koshas, the five sheaths of human being according to ancient scripture; I know the veils described in Patanjali's sutras; I know the layers of the autonomic nervous system; I know how to dance.

"There's no phone you can use here. The only phone is in the cell."

The complex process it took to move from the cell to this seat races through my mind as fast as a scent wafting past my nose—all the frisking, all the locking and unlocking, all the guard escorts. And if I lose my place in the long Commissioner line-up...

There are several women's cells, and there are male detention cells here too—Mudd had mentioned her boyfriend, his cousin, and their male friends were locked in this same building. Leaving Oz and making the trek back again is risky...

The Commissioner says I have twenty minutes.

TV's Supermarket Sweep comes to mind, the timed race of contestants through the aisles of a store, snatching foods of highest value off shelves, throwing them in carts. Except that everything is in slow motion with guards, and the only speeding is my way-too-rapidly beating heart. The guards unlock my left wrist from the table. I stand and they re-lock both wrists behind my back. They unlock and relock the solid metal door and then the wrought iron grated door. They unlock both handcuffs with my face to the wall, then arms up the wall, and pat me down. They unlock the thick cell door with a clang and send me in.

"How will I tell you when I'm ready to go back to The Commissioner?" I ask in a panic, suddenly realizing I'll be in this thick-walled, soundproof room with no communication device.

"Bang on the viewing window."

"Oh," I say.

I hadn't noticed the viewing window.

"Are you sure?" I ask my husband. Mudd's phone-smarts have finally helped me get through to him. He is sure I can tell The Commissioner my story without legal presence. We'll need a lawyer later anyhow, he says. Our conversation is curt and to-the-point. Precious minutes had perspired by with my frustrated use of this primitive phone; it is all business when I finally hear his voice.

With Mudd's help, I've slayed the witch it seems, conquered the squirming phone, the impossibly dead connection that I couldn't clear alone. I am so grateful, and I have nothing but my face to offer her. We register each other's eyes and there is so much humanity wafting between us I feel drunken, unsteady. Hugging feels beyond appropriate, but as she sends her long arms back down her sweatpants, in my mind I wrap around her. Had we acted out the moment, we would have huddled together the rest of the night and they'd have found us in the concrete corner in this way, safe and warm.

I bang on the viewing window. I am returned to The Commissioner by all the same procedures. The guards do them by rote, one tall guard whose hair is beautifully braided, is even somewhat kind, granting me the first half-smile of the night, and this time I am much less fascinated, only finding the lock-up activity ridiculous, not painful. I am passive to every pat down and click of metal on me, almost vegetative. The image of old celery comes to mind, something limp from which you might desperately try to call forth food and substance, something which is barely shape, all moisture sucked out of its strings. I recite my story to the best of my ability, but it is tricky because I still cannot believe it myself, nor can I easily separate what matters to The Commissioner from what matters to me. I have progressed a long way since my first cryptic version for Baby: "I was making hot cocoa." But there is still no more sense to the entire flash scene than there was when I first arrived. It will take years to peel back the layers of that night, though the bare-bone facts will crash down soon enough, on Tuesday.

What I do manage to articulate to The Commissioner obviously shifts something in him. He doesn't say any sympathetic words, but the ripple through his system rolls to mine like a wave. It is possible he even faces me; I believe he does in fact turn to face me. By now, I can barely look— too strong a facing, too intimate within this bastardly separation. It feels like an apology without the words, or perhaps an attempt to soften my rage, to quell my indignation when I leave here. I imagine the distress stayed with him the way ham and bologna scented my skin for days after my work shifts years ago at a London deli. I imagine it may have made him question his job, shake his head when he went home at 7:00 a.m. or whenever his wizard-work was done, and say tiredly to his wife, "I just don't know anymore... our law enforcement..."

I am free to go. Free, with the lasso of four criminal charges and the order to appear in court in several weeks. I have only to sign more papers, itself an experience of impotence. When first locked to the desk, I'd been asked if I was right or left-handed. It was a simple enough question. Yet frightening—anything about my business was frightening to reveal in this take-over setting. Why did they need to know? How detailed into my life and my body were we getting and why? The reason for the right hand / left hand question was to lock my non-dominant hand to the table, leaving the dominant one free to sign documents. Now they point to what appears to be the innards of a broken pen, the gelatinous body of a slug out of its shell. No worries that I might—might what? Stab my wrists with it? Stab a guard? Hide it in my hair the way girls did at Berkeley High, only to have ball point pen fights over boyfriends during lunch in the cafeteria? I can barely sign my name with this flaccid provision, but the quality of my signature doesn't matter, I am "free to go."

The guards double-check this. They seem surprised. The Commissioner, emotionless now, waves a hand in that discarding way one can gesture as if to say, "Take her out; be done."

I WOULD LIKE TO REPORT that things were hunky-dory from here on. But they were sad. They were distasteful, and tore at my heart. Of course I wanted to get out. But leaving the women seemed an insulting nonchalance to a friendship I wasn't sure I had claim to, one based on a most singular night of our lives. It was a time-stretched night where the need and dependence on each other for assured connection was as strong as if we'd found ourselves trapped in a cold cave against the danger of a bear. There was no future in it, no blanket to offer, no cell phones to exchange contact and email address, only the random share of this cowering moment. The eyes of each woman—Baby, Alexa, Richmond, The Social Worker, Mudd—remain in my mind like the nurse whose eyes I bored through to stay sane in my last child-birthing, whose name I never learned, whose actual face I never took in, only the eyes, not even their color, just the saving connection of them.

When I'd left the cell after the last entreaty to make a phone call, I'd turned to the women, not knowing if I would be told by The Commissioner that I would be further detained, need bail, or be un-handcuffed to go. Given the extensive criminal charges read out to me, perhaps I'd be back. But I'd wanted to say goodbye to the women if I wasn't going to see them, and I'd searched for the right way to say it. "Good luck" wouldn't work. "I will think of you" was most accurate, if I said anything, but was far too sentimental for the setting. I simply turned to look at them, and turned away, finding myself beyond words.

I was led to a bench in the hall and told to wait, that my personal items would be brought to me. Time passed, and a clear plastic bag arrived with my jacket and shoes. The pockets were empty. My other personal items, I was told, would be returned to me later. I was moved to the initial entrance room. I sat, un-handcuffed, for an unspecific span of time, waiting for questioning and further orders from "The Sergeant." Who that was, was unclear, but I wondered if it was the woman at the head desk, who was walking back and forth to the Xerox machine, occasionally making a copy while eating sunflower seeds. She split each shell delicately between her teeth, eating the seed while chatting with an employee at a smaller desk nearby. I could imagine the splitting and tiny chews kept her alert on this night shift, so, *Good for her*, I thought, ever the yoga therapist, *she might be trying to cut down on coffee.* I sat on a stool and waited, for someone to notice me, tell me a timeframe, or give me an order.

A new male was having his mugshot taken just to my right. Another male, behind jail bars along one wall, was torso-slumped over a bench, lower legs strewn on the ground. A third male was being escorted with two guards on either side holding him up: his legs did the funky chicken, his head bobbed, his eyebrows lifted as if with a question as he walked scarecrow-style in the guards' arms; his eyes squinted open, fluttered shut. He was wearing a kilt.

"We'd better get this one in a jumpsuit," one guard said to the other. "This skirt'll be way too easy to pull up."

The woman at the large desk continued her work without looking at me, and I began to doubt if it was she I was to wait for. I turned to the female guard who had told me to wait on this stool and asked if I was waiting for that person, which she confirmed. The Sergeant overheard, looked up, stared at me, and went back to her papers. Ten or fifteen minutes later, she called me and I approached her desk, but that was an error: she had only wanted me to move to a slightly closer stool. I was not to come near her desk.

The room woke up from this and looked in my direction. I'd transgressed, drawn attention now. I sat on the stool as told, about eight feet from her. She asked me several questions that were easy to answer. She asked me to recite my address.

By now I could sense that there were numerous people hanging out in the room, though I couldn't really see behind me. I was in the near center, and though the whole room was grey, I felt spotlit here in the middle; that surreal theater-in-the-round feeling again.

In my peripheral vision to the left is the guard whose kind face I'd liked. His post is quiet for the moment and he's sitting on a chair resting. One guard stands next to The Sergeant. Others I can feel and hear behind me.

I am asked again to recite my address. I am suddenly uneasy about reciting my address loud enough for The Sergeant to hear from this distance. I pause. Time ticks awkwardly. The Sergeant and I look at each other; she is expectant, she doesn't have all night. I am tongue-tied while I frantically think. My chest contracts. I am glued stuck, in my brain and on this stool.

"Did you forget your address?" she asks after too long a pause.

"No, I didn't forget my address."

I don't want to appear suspicious, as if I'm trying to make up a different address or some such, or as if I'm trying to recall a false address I'd told earlier. As it is, my last name is not my legal name, though it is on my driver's license and my credit cards, bank account, check book. It is my grandmother's name I took thirty years ago, finding it both beautiful and more representative of me than my grandfather's. I am hoping I won't now be nailed by this failing to come clean with the complexity of my name. Little do I know that the cops have misspelled my name on the report, so that my criminal record isn't even accurately me—with any of my names. What matters is I don't want to irritate The Sergeant in my last breath before exiting, but there's no perfect way to say why I've paused.

"I don't wish to speak it loudly," I say quietly. "My address, that is." I don't want to offend anyone, but I feel unsafe shouting my address in this room on this night. She graciously tells me to approach the desk to recite my address, which I do.

With a loud thump, she stamps several documents, and I am dismissed. I receive my personal items—a hair clip, earrings, a tiny moonstone necklace by Julia Szendrei bought at the San Francisco airport after my stepmother's funeral. This necklace will become the one piece I wear for more than a year after this night, when my face is red-streaked, my hair falls out, my ears remain inflamed and my pierced earring holes are swollen shut, disallowing my go-to of earrings. This twenty-eight-dollar necklace will help in so many ways.

A guard is called to escort me out. As I am led to the door, the kind guard with braids speaks. His cheek is turned to me so I can't fully see his face, yet he speaks loud enough so I can hear, and clearly he is angry that I was reluctant to share my address.

"Yup, she's worried about us," he says, emphasizing *us*.

The room turns to me, eight or nine faces funnel toward the single exit. The guard and newly arrested male doing thumbprints freeze in action and swivel their spines. It is a still-life photo moment, as if I'd requested them to "look at the camera." Had I insulted the incoming handcuffed men? The drunkard in a kilt? The slumbering man strewn sacked over a bench behind bars? The several guards on and off duty hanging out in this one "social" room?

His anger hits me like a final slap. I haven't slept since Thursday and this is Saturday morning. I haven't had a sip of water or the touch of a hand through this whole ordeal. My contact lenses scratch with every blink and my vision is a blur. My body is raging and frozen, my skin is swollen, every limb trembles. I had been warmed by the face of this one man. It was his sole smile with every lock up; it was he who saw me ill and suggested a nurse. Now the face is sour, resentful. No longer the lowly prisoner he felt sympathy for, I am the privileged white woman they are letting go. Suddenly I am uppity, wanting my stuff, asking who I am waiting for, wanting to pronounce my street number quietly. Suddenly I am the one leaving. It is his work place I've insulted, and he isn't free to go.

"Yup, now we're all going to show up at her house and rob her," he says.

I want to say so many things. I want to say, *That's already been done tonight.* I want to say, *Yes, I don't feel one dime safe here to spout my address.*

I stand at the door, too tired to say anything bright or home-run-ish. I turn my whole body and look straight at him. My voice is caught and hoarse.

"Good night, sir," I say.

The guard assigned to exit me slammed the first door we passed through, with that familiar resounding clang, and we continued alone. Half outside, we came to a locked wall and the guard told me to turn my head left. He pressed four digits for a code. The wall slid open to his touch and clanged behind us as we passed. We came to a wrought iron gate, big enough for an army truck to pass through when open.

"Turn your head left," the guard ordered again, before punching in a code for the gate.

I hesitated for a second. Eye contact. Then I turned my head.

"Interesting isn't it, that my desire to keep my address private was insulting," I said with my head turned, "but your desire to keep your code private is considered reasonable." My throat was becoming half-unglued; I'd have to watch it.

On the other side of the iron gate was a road that led up hill to a parking lot. It was pitch black at 4:30 a.m. No one was around. I had no clue where I was. My husband was supposed to come get me, but would he find me? I had no cell phone, no ID, no money, no food, no water, I couldn't see, my words barely came out, my legs barely walked.

"You are not going to leave me here, really? Are you?" I asked. "I mean, really…I'm locked up because I'm a criminal, and now you're going to release me out here alone with no way to contact anyone and no assurance that anyone will find me to pick me up?"

"You can wait in the lobby," he said.

There was nothing but the prison driveway in sight. "Where is the lobby?"

"It's up that sidewalk and then to your right," he said, pointing into the dark toward something out of our sight that I had to trust was there, up the hill and around the corner.

"No," I said. "I am not walking by myself to some lobby I can't see, that might be locked or that I can't find, and then stand out here alone in no-man's land in the middle of the night."

The guard walked me to the lobby, unlocked it, and left. I waited there with two male strangers, who presumably had also just been released from the jail, until my husband, who indeed got lost trying to find this secluded place, arrived.

I did not smile. I got into the back seat and spoke not at all.

INTERMEZZO 6

Full Circle

THREE DAYS HAVE PASSED SINCE I've been home, three nights of nightmares and crying, with one span of levity while walking the dog with my son when he reported that most of his high school, thanks to social media, circulated the news that I single-handedly "took down some cops." It is Tuesday morning and I am yet again sobbing in bed, held by my husband who doesn't care that he'll be late for a meeting.

Our friend, Matthew, arrives in a suit to pick up Robin, and I answer the door. Together they'll drive downtown for their appointment. I have made Robin late, and he calls downstairs to me and Matthew to say he'll be right there. Matthew and I are chatting. It's been too long since our families have visited, at least a couple of months. Matthew and Elena's son, Mateo, entered our elementary school in third grade and we've enjoyed the family for ten years since. They live half a mile away.

"How've you been?" he asks.

"Hmmm, so-so," I say. "I'll tell you about it another time." I want to spill all, but it is too long a story for suited men heading out to present a proposal downtown. It takes a lot to get my husband to wear a tie, but this is Washington D.C. we're talking about, and he is wearing one.

Matthew and I talk about the vegetable garden he planted with painstaking care on the side of our house, since we have sun and their house is shaded by the tall oaks of Sligo Creek. Sadly, his garden here, so well-tended in orderly plots with stakes and strings and cups cut to protect seedlings, has not succeeded. Our own sunlight changed after our neighbors expanded their house, and the side plot that once produced huge zucchini and tomatoes treated Matthew's plants to mold.

I sort Hallowe'en candy as we chat. Mostly the dregs of yellow and green Starbursts are left at the bottom of my ghost bucket, but surprisingly there are also Mounds bars and Butterfingers. "Not as many trick-or-treaters this year," I say, pointing to the leftovers. "I think because of the construction across the street, so the corner is dark."

"We didn't get as many trick-or-treaters either," he says. "Actually, all in all, it wasn't a good Hallowe'en."

"I agree with that," I say, keeping my story to myself for now. Not only is it too big an event to tell quickly, but the lawyer we'd seen Monday morning told us not to speak of it until my case was cleared—*if* he was able to clear it. "The more word gets around," he'd said, "the more it forces the police on the defensive. The charges could end with a jail sentence," he'd said. "Keep quiet, leave it to me, don't take chances."

But, why wasn't *their* Hallowe'en good? I wonder, and ask Matthew.

"Mateo was mugged," Matthew answers.

Mateo had been trick-or-treating with his friend, Steve, when fifteen youths came out of the trees by the elementary school and demanded Steve's cell phone. Steve, who, at age seventeen is 6'6", refused to give up his phone and was knocked down with a 2x4 board, something like a wooden slat from a fence. Twice.

When the gang demanded Mateo's cell, he said, "Sure." It had been 10:00 at night. They reported it to the police.

Our incident a half-mile away began around 10:30.

The elder, bald cop from our backyard scene had followed our son and his two friends thinking they were part of the gang who'd assaulted Mateo and Steve. The cop had seen our boys, in costumes, when they left our yard briefly; they'd been walking to their friend's car to get a connecting wire for the party sound equipment. The elder cop, in an undercover car, watched them, saw them pass what he thought looked like a 2x4 on the ground, and called for backup as he monitored them entering our backyard through the alley. Seven cops had burst through our gate.

I immediately call Elena. Matthew's wife and I have become warm friends over the years, showing mutual kindness through both families' financial struggles, aging and dying parents, rearing teens, and my husband's incapacitating knee replacement, during which Elena's spanakopita and raw beet salad were gifts. I know she is good for some details. She tells me they reported the assault, Steve had gone home to his parents' care, and Mateo was taken to the police station to identify the young man who had his wallet.

There had been about fifteen young adults, she confirmed, as Mateo had told the police. Some wore ski masks.

Ski masks...like my son's Ninja costume, carefully planned out when we sorted through every winter hat and balaclava to find the right costume look.

All were dressed in black. Not all in the gang approved of the aggression, however. One or two individuals discouraged it saying, "Oh, come on" and "Hey, let's go."

All were male, Elena said. Except one. They went to that one woman's house afterward and that's where they were all arrested, some firearms found too.

"There was one female?" I asked. I was starting to feel strange—dizzy and clear all at once.

"Yes, but she wasn't really part of it. She stayed in the distance. 'Come on, let's go, come on, leave them alone,' she'd said from behind some trees."

Later that night the woman was taken in.

She was put in a cold cell with five other women—a teen who'd beaten a bully schoolgirl, a cheerful Latina with a violent ex who'd had her arrested for assault, a sex worker from Richmond, California, a social worker who hadn't paid her speeding tickets, and a sixty-year-old mom who was tackled by police after they took three kids from her yard thinking they were the ones who'd assaulted their own friends.

Her name was Mudd.

She had her arms down her sweatpants and she was kind.

ACKNOWLEDGMENTS

Thank you, Mary Partlow for saying, *Write!* when I told you writing was keeping me sane. Those notes began this book.

Thank you, Betty Sitka, for our counseling exchanges in your safe presence.

Thank you, Rachel Pentlarge, for helping us counsel on that first day.

Thank you, Pam Dillon of Salt Spring Island, Canada, for helping my husband and me through our break and into repair.

Thank you, Darian Unger, for active listening, suggestions, and respect, especially to our son.

Thank you, Lyn Stone, for your cartoons, and your counseling while we froze and walked our dogs. You were one person who saw just how much trouble I was in.

Thank you, Elizabeth (Lisa) Null, for offering support in our appeal to the County Executive for de-escalation training and body cameras.

Thank you, Flora, for the kindest heart and the softest hands.

Thank you, Robin the Woman, for your Seeing and your touch.

Thank you, Wendy Rothenberg, for the sisterhood of watching that thirty-second video together.

Thank you, Linda Bendor, for late phone calls as I tried to make sense of what happened.

Thank you, Nancy Tepperman, for connecting me to Ms. La Don.

Thank you, Josh Bendor, for your ACLU know-how and long-distance advice.

Thank you to my siblings—Linda, Nancy, Larry, Jeff, Wendy—for rooting for me.

Thank you, Jane Redmont, for one sentence that may have helped me more than any other.

Thank you, Dr. Christina Steele, extraordinary biodynamic osteopath, for helping my nervous system, pelvis, shoulders, knees, and heart.

Thank you to these people for hosting my workshops, trainings, or presentations: Wendy Bonvechio of Secret Garden Yoga; Ashley Sky Litecky, Angelique Raptakis, and Katie Presley of Sky House Yoga; Joe Miller, Natalie Miller, Heidi Scanlon, Erin Pendergrass, Veda Darling, and Lori Wilen of Willow Street Yoga Center; Aimee McBride and Irene Glasse of Shala Wellness Center; Monya Cohen of the John L. Gildner Regional Institute for Children and Adolescents; Julia Romano of Em-Power Yoga and Chris Parkison of Vida Fitness; Lori Bashour and Michael Lee at the Phoenix Rising Yoga Therapy Practitioners Conference.

Acknowledgments

Thank you, Joe Miller, Director of Willow Street Yoga for inviting the launch of my first book, and Erin Pendergrass, manager, who helped make it happen. Thank you to every attendee.

Thank you to Grace Yoga for the glorious space to see my clients.

Thank you, Laurie Hyland Robertson, a visionary editor, for publishing my article in Yoga Therapy Today, and former editor Kelly Birch, for initial stage efforts.

Thank you to every workshop participant in my acute trauma care professional trainings for your passion and your application of this work with survivors of trauma and assault.

Thank you, yoga therapist Dawn Valentine, for your beautiful assistance in the 2019-20 training.

Thank you, Angela Grice, for presenting your valuable work at the last workshop, and Jennifer Brennan, Hannah Davis, and Angelique Raptakis for your support.

Thank you, Francine Brungardt, for standing in for me at the Book Fair while I was teaching.

Thank you, Vicki, Colleen, Linda, Gail, Olga, Joanne, Royal, Karen, Patricia, Kira, and Katy Rose Cooke, who contributed to the launch of the Ella's Gift Fund, helping to provide scholarships for assault survivors to receive yoga therapy sessions, and for deserving professionals to attend my workshops.

Thank you to all who purchased my previous book, *SURVIVING ASSAULT: Words that Rock & Quiet & Tell the Truth*, proceeds of which go to this scholarship fund.

Thank you to all who contributed to the GoFundMe page and performance in 2018. I am so appreciative—you actually facilitated the publication of this book.

Thank you to the beautiful artists who performed with me for this fundraiser: Margaret Iki Riddle, dancer; Sarah Hippert, aerialist; Kelly Denson, speaker.

Thank you, Jess Hoover, audio-visual technician; Angela Grice, announcer; Belinda Lee, Jasmine La Flor, Mabelyn Mijangos, stage support; and Sky House for the beautiful space.

Thank you Erik Lewis for hopping on your bike, driving from Brooklyn to Manhattan, borrowing a camera, biking back to Brooklyn, getting in your car and driving to Maryland, to film my fundraiser show at the last minute when I was stuck.

Thank you, Katie Randall, who stabilized me during graduate school lectures when triggers threatened my sanity.

Thank you, Julia Romano, for belief when I didn't think I'd make it.

Thank you, Shelley Gilbertson Goldman, Denyse Patterson, and Kim Metz, for partnering me when I knew what to do but didn't have the hands to do it. Thank you, Shelley at the helm. Those charted practices are in Appendix II.

Thank you, Rosita Larrain of Salt Spring Island, for creating and dancing together, and for your work with women in need.

Thank you, Sura Kim, for your cottage as a base, and your gifts of teaching meditation to the world: suraflow.org

Thank you, Dennis Redmont, for the generosity of your apartment where several chapters were drafted.

Thank you, Deborah Kaplan, for fifty years of friendship, which provided me safe focus.

Thank you, Gael Pardi, for keeping your eyes on me always, and for your gifts as a reader.

Thank you, Carolyn Bluemle, for your belief in my writing and my teaching.

Thank you, Sharon Javna, my comrade since MLK Jr. High.

Thank you, Linda Cinciotta Olguin, for your notes and the statue that brought me strength and solace.

Thank you, Gail Fisher. For fighting for me.

Thank you, Colleen Bergeron, for your smile and for excel spreadsheets that made life simple.

Thank you, Susan Jay Rounds, and Raul Ramirez's reporting class at SF State.

Thank you, Vicki Berman, for all your support to me and your work with others in need.

Thank you, Rick Kowalewski, for your Monday morning yin yoga class after which I'd hole up in Starbucks and write for five hours.

Thank you, Anne Esguerra, who I met years later while assisting at a Phoenix Rising Yoga Therapy Training, and who I knew, finally, was someone who could hold my story with unblinking strength. Our session together will be published in a separate piece on *Presence*. A gifted yoga therapist: www.integrativelifetherapy.com

Thank you to all the neighbors mentioned in the Silent Vigil chapter. You signed your name and you showed up on those cold nights.

Thank you, mama bear Carol Radomski, for twenty-eight years of friendship and trust.

Thank you, Maria Kardamaki, and Simone Scupi for good walks, and even laughter.

Thank you, J. Sera Crandall, for great intelligence discussing the polyvagal theory.

Thank you, Phoenix Rising Yoga Therapy, and Re-Evaluation Counseling, two humble and profound modalities. These are tools all practitioners should have, and all humans deserve.

Thank you, Doreen Cantor Paster, Lora Griff, Marla Zipin, Phil Zipin, and Paul Taskier for your help.

Thank you, Melissa Bannett, for accompanying me to the county executive's meeting.

Thank you, Jennifer Parker of Sedona for your seeing ahead.

Thank you, Ebonye Gussine Wilkins, for sharing your knowledge.

Thank you, Cecelia E. Reed and Trina Burpo, for confirming early childhood history and for sharing your most precious mother and grandmother with me.

Thank you, Deborah King, Susannah Numa, La Don Williams, and Akosua Anum Yeboah for your skilled and sensitive readings of early drafts. Your contributions were so helpful.

Thank you, Lorna Jane Cook, gifted author and sage advisor, for every detail you helped with. Your next novel can't come soon enough.

Thank you, Mary Carpenter for coaching that was tough and true; the effects lie deep in the pages of this book.

Thank you, Debbie Weingarten, award-winning writer, activist, coach, editor, advocate. Any writer who wants a partner in their writing process need look no further. www.cactuswrenwriting.com

Thank you, stellar book designer, artist, and publication mentor, Sarah Lahay of C'est Beau Designs. You were patient through a pandemic and national crises. I look forward to manifesting the next book; it's waiting. www.cestbeaudesigns.com

Thank you, Professor Thomas Nassif, for guidance in writing a self-case report.

Thank you, Professor James Snow, for legitimizing the idea of a self-case report.

Thank you, Professor Marlysa Sullivan, for your wisdom when I was in pain.

Thank you, Professor Kirsten Pullin for true words.

Thank you, Maryland University of Integrative Health, for the award honoring my work in acute trauma care. That might have meant even more to me than my degree.

Thank you, Amy Cruise of the Maryland ACLU. Thank you to the ACLU period.

Thank you, Maria Hamilton, for your call to action, organizing the small but passionate 2015 Million Moms March. Your brave voice gave us voice: mothersforjusticeunited.org

Thank you, Kelly McGraw (Kali). Somewhere in the rewrite of our ancestry, we are sisters, having survived similar affronts in different cities.

Thank you to my parents who lived their short lives with integrity, kindness, and risk.

Thank you to my son, Daniel. For reading rough drafts and endorsing them. For asking for more. For your artistry. For the passionate person you are and how we all knew that if you'd been there, you wouldn't have been able to control yourself from jumping in, and how we love you for that.

Thank you to my son, Mikhael, for educating yourself about the world without any help from us. For knowing how the system works, sticking your neck out dangerously, and in so doing, saving my ass from jail. Thank you for your equal parts humor and love.

Thank you to my husband, Robin. You are soft and genius; you are generous and visionary. You have hung in there when our lights were out and there was no path forward.

To all who listen well to another; to all who see another's strength and courage; to all who lend themselves in darkest times: Thank You.

APPENDIX I

SUGGESTED RESOURCES:

I value these resources, and collectively they've added to the knowledge behind my work.

1. Phoenix Rising Yoga Therapy:
    http://pryt.com/pryt-directory/

2. TED talk with Kelly McGonigal, 2013 — important reframing of the stress response:
    https://www.ted.com/talks/kelly_mcgonigal_how_to_make_stress_your_friend#t-723954

3. The 3 Diaphragms Model with Matthew Taylor — connecting the dots from big toe to brain:
    https://www.youtube.com/watch?v=HTkFuPLZ3Uk

4. "A New Normal: Ten Things I've Learned About Trauma," by Catherine Woodiwiss, *Sojourners* Magazine:
    https://sojo.net/articles/new-normal-ten-things-ive-learned-about-trauma

5. Helpful guidance about the trauma of sexual or violent assault:
    http://satchawaii.com/get-help/dealing-with-trauma-of-sexual-assault//

6. "A Survivor's Life," by Eli Saslow — unsparing and accurate profile of the acute stage after trauma: http://www.washingtonpost.com/sf/national/2015/ 12/05/after-a-mass-shooting-a-survivors-life/?utm_ term=.5ed26c59306c

7. Nadia Murad — victim of Isis torture in 2014, and Nobel Peace Prize winner in 2018, now defends others: https://www.glamour.com/story/women-of-the-year- nadia-murad

8. R.A.I.N. (Recognize, Allow, Investigate, Nourish) meditations with Tara Brach — Working with Difficulties: https://www.tarabrach.com/articles-interviews/ rainworkingwithdifficulties/

   R.A.I.N. meditations with Tara Brach — On Self Compassion: http://www.tarabrach.com/wp-content/uploads/pdf/ RAINof-Self-Compassion2.pdf

APPENDIX II

Yoga Therapy as Complementary Early Intervention for the Acute Stage Following Assault or Trauma (Adapted from a self-case report)

by Diana Tokaji, M.Sc., C-IAYT, E-RYT500, PRYT .
Unpublished. May 2014.

AN ASSAULT IS SHOCKING AND violating by nature and may rupture a person's connectivity to body, mind, and world. This I discovered when I was victim to an unpredictable assault, an experience that would lead me to respect early intervention as both essential and its own specific art. I had thought I understood how to work with trauma, having navigated steadily through the physical and mental effects of my own life experiences and having worked with private clients for many years. But I discovered that my system, so rattled to the core by this assault, deserved fresh respect, and I had to step out of the way of my own preconceptions for it to teach me.

One year after the assault, I wrote a self-case report which became the base for workshops I offer to professionals in our and related fields, and which is the background for my commentary here. A literature search had revealed rich return on the topic of posttraumatic stress disorder, and the efficacy of various techniques—including yoga—for recovery. (Streeter et al., 2012) But results were scant for the acute stage post-assault. During the trial and error period after the assault, I had kept track of my early practices—those that failed horribly and those that worked. This grew into the mentored self-case report on early intervention, with simple protocols I came to value: therapeutic yoga practices for grounding my system and spirit, for deflecting negativity, and for accessing wisdom so necessary for my survival.

The assault and its aftermath were like a rupture to multiple layers of my being. On a physical and energetic plane, my musculoskeletal and nervous systems were obviously and immediately affected, and still require care two years later. More subtle but perhaps more prevalent, was the "moral injury"— as coined by trauma scholar Jonathan Shay—the particular psychological harm of an assault, the loss of faith in the world, the breach of trust, shame and self-blame, and ensuing fears. His words confirm what is a complex healing process, and not likely to be a singular event.

Indeed, secondary and tertiary assaults shook me in the wake of the primary, with medical and orthopedic problems, mental instability, legal fees, threatening court dates, loss of executive function, marital issues, work loss, financial stress, social isolation. As well, constant triggers re-stimulated the primary assault, life-threatening events that occurred without predictability in a car, a store, or a darkened yoga class. In the language of the *panchamaya kosha*, all five sheaths—physical body, breath, mind state, wisdom body, and bliss—were disturbed. Well-meaning friends and colleagues referred to "healing" and "recovery." But I was in survival, a juncture between living and giving up that required courage and immense will. I turned to my inner wisdom layer, *vijnanamaya kosha*, with ferocity; and to strength-based practices.

Strength-focused grounding interventions (Chan et al., 2006) contradict the extreme state of vulnerability, fear, and hyper-arousal following an assault, sensations that incite a victim to wish to flee body and world as both become foci of pain. I did not immediately know this however. I'd learned to trust my forty years of intuitive practices, called upon at many crossroads when my personal history of loss or my physical disabilities confounded me. But after the assault, I would find to my costly surprise, that to rally against the darkness overpowering me, to garner strength and wisdom, I had to do a yoga practice that was, at least at first, completely counter-intuitive. I knew that a bottom-up approach (Taylor et al., 2010), where visceral activities send messages from the periphery to the brain, could override my cognitive disrepair at least temporarily, buying me moments of clarity. And I knew that I would simultaneously need a top-down approach of intentional mental focus to reduce autonomic reactivity (Gard et al., 2014), at a time when my body was freakishly out of control. Somewhere in the decades of practice I harbored a knowing that amounted to this: grounding the body, witness-consciousness, connectivity (to human, animal, nature), and meaningful action in the world (Poulin et al., 2013; McGonigal, 2013) would root me to rise. But first I'd make mistakes.

ASSAULT AND REACTION

On October 31, 2014, I experienced an immediate eruption of physical and mental health symptoms in response to a traumatic event. The event involved excessive force by multiple police officers on my person, followed by traumatic incarceration for one night, and the threat of up to thirteen years imprisonment upon release. To summarize the many twists and turns, my "case" was eventually expunged without penalty.

Symptoms of distress erupted within a half hour of the assault during forced incarceration, when extreme heat and inflammation of my ears and facial skin occurred despite the freezing environment. This was accompanied by tachycardia, shortness of breath, and severe trembling. Extreme dehydration followed, such that I had to peel my lips from my teeth to speak; my vision was blurred and blinking was painful.

In the days and weeks that followed, I experienced changeable knee pain, my right, then both knees, and was unable to descend stairs. I had pelvic pain, with no problem found by the doctor. Extreme heat, inflammation and redness of my ears and face cycled repeatedly into a skin condition. Nightmares, heightened anxiety, panic from bright lights, inability to make decisions, and morbid thoughts were constant.

BACKGROUND

At the time of the incident, which took place outside our family home of twenty-five years, I was sixty years old, had been married for thirty-four years, and was the mother of twenty-three- and seventeen-year-old sons, the latter of whom was present and videotaped the assault. I was in sound physical and mental health, did not drink or smoke, took no medications, had no criminal record, and in a journal entry four days prior to the assault, spoke of my "vitality."

Using self-care to treat symptoms is common to me. I began working solo to solve my physical problems when I was eighteen. In 1983, I became a certified Integral Yoga teacher with Nischala Joy Devi, and for thirty years thereafter, studied structurally-focused yoga styles with master Iyengar and Anusara teachers. In 1997, I graduated as a Level III practitioner of Phoenix Rising Yoga Therapy, work that would further support my ability to resolve body/mind issues through exploration and self-inquiry. I am a certified Relax and Renew trainer with Judith Lasater and completed her advanced training in restorative yoga. I am a certified Pilates mat instructor since 1999. I have been a peer counselor in Re-evaluation Counseling (RC) for ten years.

SUPPORT AND ISOLATION

In addition to yoga, supports I had in place included a cranial-sacral osteopath, and my RC co-counseling partner, for bi-monthly session exchanges of attentive listening and discharging of emotion. I did not take medication; I did take Bach Flower "Rescue" Remedy, although with no seeming affect.

My husband and son at home were sources of both support and of contention, as they loved me but they handled their rage over what happened by shutting it out, something I could not do. My husband stepped in as main parent and grocery shopped for a year due to my trigger from bright lights in stores. The most pronounced improvement to my inflamed ears and skin condition occurred one year after the assault, when my husband and I spent a week at a silent retreat.

I am a writer, dancer, and choreographer, though at the time of the assault, my artistic work was on hold. I was in year two of graduate school in yoga therapy at Maryland University of Integrative Health (MUIH), and also continued to see private clients with a variety of conditions as I had for seventeen years. The school environment accelerated my training in self-reflection, musculoskeletal assessment, neuroscience, and the tools of yoga therapy for healing. In one instance, a 15-second conversation with my mentor in the yoga therapy clinic led to solving pain symptoms. To my question about the pelvic pain I was experiencing, Marlysa Sullivan gently asked "How long since you were assaulted?" a reply that took me to my yoga mat, to self-inquiry, intuitive practices, and resolution of pain.

School also heightened my awareness of the destructive effects of stress on the system, which ironically became an intense source of additional stress. With my face and ears already inflamed from sympathetic nervous system hyper-arousal, I sat through terrifying lectures and discussions about the latest medical research—studies that showed how the chemical surge occurring within me, could be permanently punishing: "Stress and its related hormones epinephrine and norepinephrine play a crucial role in tumor progression." (Qin et al., 2015) And I learned about the next layer of irony, found in recent studies in psychology: "The *perception* that stress is damaging may further a stressed person's stress response. Individuals who perceived that stress affects their health and reported a large amount of stress had an increased risk of premature death." (Keller et al., 2015)

At MUIH, our cohort learned about new stress reduction programs using yoga and mindfulness meditation with members of law enforcement. A Virginia chief of police and her deputy sergeant shared three hours of emotional testimony about PTSD in the force and the debilitating effects of job-related stress. Afterwards, we chanted "OM" and hugs were exchanged. This unusually human interaction with armed, uniformed officers may have tinted my view when I encountered seven male and female police in my backyard several months later. I saw them as normal people and expected them to treat me with respect. My background as a daughter of pacifists, who shielded us from cop shows and disallowed squirt guns, added to my cultural ignorance of law and order.

Our graduate school program director, Mary Partlow, extended my due dates for all school assignments to eliminate the pressure as I awaited my court date. She understood that writing was a healing art for me, and she encouraged that priority. This was vital to my road to better health.

The lawyer told us not to speak about our case until it was closed, a two-month period of near-secrecy. Civilian deaths by police were in the national news, with video footage that was frighteningly familiar. I didn't fit the typical profile for police brutality, however, and people I shared my story with were often skeptical. Once I was able to speak out, with each meaningful action I undertook—testifying before the Maryland State Senate, marching with mothers for police body cameras and de-escalation training, I experienced a surge of improved well-being.

My community activities proved both altruistic and beneficial to my health. Oxytocin, produced under stress but also from positive human connection—touch, warmth, psychological support—has "stress-buffering and restorative properties that are responsible, at least in part, for health and longevity benefits associated with helping others." (Brown, 2015) More dramatically, "Providing help to others predicts a reduced association between stress and mortality." (Poulin et al., 2013) Kelly McGonigal's TED talk, 2013, which opens with her apology for espousing the negative health effects of stress, and ends with pronouncement that our wise bodies have equal access to neurohormones of healing, lifted a weight from my shoulders and helped me breathe.

TRIAL AND ERROR YOGA PRACTICES

On November 2, the day after I was released from jail, I did an intuitive yoga practice alone, prior to joining family at my son's soccer game. I moved gently owing to stiffness, gradually my spine warmed up, and I was drawn to backbend into *ustrasana* (camel pose). After this expansive chest-opening posture, I did a long dog pose, a twist, and took a few quiet moments drinking in a surprisingly warm November sun. I got up feeling nourished by my practice. I changed my clothes and picked up my keys.

As I neared the front door to leave, a wave of sensation overcame me. I can best describe it like an east coast storm—dark clouds blackening a sky that had demanded sunglasses only moments before. My legs buckled beneath me. I began to gag while sobbing. My windpipe narrowed and I struggled to breathe.

I fell to the floor and felt vomit rise, with it a fear that I was going to choke. I crawled to my phone and dialed a neighbor friend. I had not yet told her what had happened and communicated with difficulty. She understood to rush over and I fell into her arms.

On November 3, I did a second intuitive practice. I avoided backbends, thinking that my sympathetic nervous system might have been stimulated by the deep motion of the thoracic spine, and that a heart-opening camel pose might have been premature after the contractual effect of an assault and jail. Instead, I surmised, my body desired an inward folding, protective motions such as forward bends—*uttanasana, paschimotanasana, baddha konasana.* These felt wonderful. Then *adho mukha svanasana* (dog pose). Slowly and mindfully I folded into *balasana,* the pose of the child. I had begun to enjoy a deepening breath when the same wave of sensation returned—blackening clouds overtaking the sun, this time a darkness encroaching up my back and over my head. Instantly I recognized the sign and ran from the deck where I was practicing into the house and my husband's arms, where, as before, I began to shake, choke, collapse, as if I had no legs. My husband held me up. I now understood that the trigger was not simply opening my chest, but this:

1. I had been kicked to my knees by the most aggressive policeman, and while physical problems with my knees wouldn't show up for a number of weeks, physical recall of the assault was sharp to that moment. Using methods of self-inquiry and self-integration from Phoenix Rising Yoga Therapy, and the Buddhist-derived mindfulness technique of R.A.I.N. from meditation teacher Tara Brach – **R**ecognize, **A**llow, **I**nvestigate, **N**ourish – I realized that standing on my knees in both camel and child's pose were sensory triggers.

2. An absence of vigilance occurred in both poses. In camel, my head was arched back to the sky; in child's, my head was bowed to the ground. The directions were opposite but consistent: movement of head and eyes in both cases was away from center to an extreme, eliciting primal feelings of vulnerability and powerlessness.

3. Expansion. Whether extension or flexion, both the backbend of camel and the forward fold of child's pose created qualities of expansion. The expansive nature of both extension and flexion was not safe.

4. Autonomic Nervous System activation. I'd previously had a simplified bad guy/good guy image of the sympathetic and parasympathetic nervous systems (SNS, PNS). Now I suspected a scenario that was nuanced. Maybe splanchnic nerve innervation from doing camel pose cranked up the SNS; maybe dorsal vagal stimulation from child's pose activated the PNS with too much speed, screech-stopping the sympathetic while setting off the immobilizing dorsal vagal response of *collapse*, akin to "playing dead" in the animal world. If this theory was true, it explained why twice during and after my post-assault yoga practices my legs gave way beneath me: *The release that came with increased parasympathetic activity was no safer for me now than the uplift that came with increased sympathetic.*

I was determined to find practices that would allow my body expression and positive sensation and would move me toward homeostasis while avoiding trigger. I knew I wouldn't bow my head forward or back. I would have my feet on the ground. Although

I hadn't suffered sexual assault, my body had been overpowered and treated brutally, and because it registered as violation, I would be keeping my stance narrow and my legs parallel. I knew that although my training in restorative poses had taught me "warm, dark, quiet," I would need cool to heat the *rajas* I was suffering, and light, not dark, was my peace, since I was assaulted at night. The light could not be direct in my eyes I would find out, as this was an immediate trigger to a high beam flashlight the police had shined, blinding my vision.

I knew not to be alone in the house while I practiced. I had to firmly press extremities to stable surfaces—hands and feet, of course, but also by pressing on my own crown, my own iliac crests, my own thighs. *Closed kinetic chain* was something I would create either physically by myself, by using imagery, or later in assist exchanges with colleagues. Quadriceps engagement, I had learned from Heather Mason of The Minded Institute, London, were key to stability when working with acute anxiety, the state that I was in. Every pose for now used muscular engagement. Later, I would add a heavy dose of gluteus medius engagement to stabilize my knees.

As can happen following an assault, my fears were not only a reaction to what had shockingly occurred but reflected concerns for my uncertain future. Although I'd filed a complaint to the Internal Affairs Division, I would need, literally and figuratively, two legs to stand on to fight the criminal charges against me. This ongoing absence of safety is important to understand, as it is often the reality for a survivor of trauma, abuse, or assault. There was no "post-assault" as found in PTSD's, *post assault* stress disorder. Rather, the absence of safety was real and continuous. I created practices that were simple but extraordinary in effect. There was no panacea, no eraser of the horror implanted in brain and body, but these practices innervated temporary strength without activation. Here are the premises I arrived at—building blocks for safe physical practices:

ELEMENTS OF PRACTICE

Vigilance

Symmetry

Narrow stance

Knees parallel

Closed kinetic chain

Heels on earth

Quadriceps engaged

Eyes open

Head level

Protective Mudra

EFFECTS AND CREATIVE APPLICATIONS

The first of four practices I developed can be found in the following chart. I trusted my body with these simple, strength-focused practices, and when I adhered strictly to the ten *Elements of Practice* above, I was not triggered. These safe actions toned my muscles toward center, inspired axial length, and created positive sensation while remaining vigilant to danger. Afterwards, I could modulate my energy in contrast to the random currents at other times. I had safe emotional releases during these practices, and they bought me two or three hours of executive function. Grounding the physical *annamaya kosha* layer was a zipline to the wisdom sheath for me, where I found inner guidance.

I repeated all or segments of Practice 1 (see chart) for a week, and sometimes repeatedly throughout the day to stabilize as needed. My subsequent practices carefully evolved from the same *Elements of Practice* themes, gradually widening in scope as safety permitted. This strength-based, quadriceps-engaged protocol was a guide, a template; it didn't change the reality of the assault, nor its damaging effect. But it oriented me to my physical midline, invoking brief, safe intervals of courage and clarity from which I could act.

Since introducing these principles, other practitioners have used them with: cancer patients (both illness and treatment can register as assault); juvenile girls in outpatient care and teens in restrictive residencies (youth with traumatic histories); female prison inmates (trauma history plus powerlessness); psychotherapy clients (using verbal and visual cues but no touch);

and during actual assaults (when the near-victims called up this physical anchoring and with aggressive stance verbally attacked their attackers). Later, this protocol helped these women in reclaiming equilibrium.

In addition to using these practices still for my recovery, I use them at intervals to stave off trigger, to re-ground when national or personal news terrifies me, to rally strength when I'm witness to a client's tough story, and to override negativity so I can accomplish challenging tasks, such as speaking out for police reform, writing the truth, or returning to strong center when harshness has hit.

The mudras suggested here and additional ones recommended in my book, *SURVIVING ASSAULT: Words that Rock & Quiet & Tell the Truth—Resource for the Living*, were invaluable and continue to be so, moment by moment, providing me strength and faith. They have proven profoundly useful for clients.

PRACTICE 1: *Tether to the Earth*

Pose	Description	Cues	Assists
1. Chair Sit Seated, place hands on arm rests or make soft fists face down on thighs (*Adhi Mudra*). Other options: palms weighting thighs, palms on chest or belly, or *Kanishtha Sharira Mudra*, weighting iliac crests (hips). *Connection to the earth*	Sit midway or to front of seat with thighs just higher than knees (add blanket to seat if needed; place books under feet if they don't reach the floor).	Feet firm to earth. Eyes open. Symmetrical head and eyes (option to slowly scan horizon). *Feel weight in heels, balls of feet; in sitting bones. Spine as strong pillar: light coursing through.*	Many options: 1.Firmly press heels. 2.Use sandbags or press forearm on thighs. 3.Press hands on iliac crests of hips. 4.Flat palm between shoulder blades. 5.Firm hands to shoulders tops. 6.One hand presses to crown of head.

Pose	Description	Cues	Assists
2. Fierce Pose with Svasti Mudra *Gesture of wellbeing for protection from negative energy.*	Stand with feet hip width apart or most solid stance. Bend knees. Forearms crisscross in front of chest, wrists flexed, palms face out, closed webs.	*Feel feet firm to earth. Belly deep. Hips strong, legs strong. Crown tall. Press cross point of forearms into each other, noting power in the back.*	Press client's heels or ankles to earth. Client chooses a focal point. Can imagine positive resource to "see" while in this pose. Or if safe, can "see" the negative energy and stop it.
3. Mountain Pose Standing: *I am here.*	Feet hip width apart. Explore arm choices e.g., palms out in *stop* or other powerful gesture.	*I am here. I am on this earth.*	Palm or block to crown. Or press heels/ankles. With 2+ practitioners, use multiple assists for responsive upward motion while grounding.

Pose	Description	Cues	Assists
4. Standing Dog *Connected*	Choose safe space: palms press on table, counter, or window ledge. Walk feet back to form an angle, heels firm to ground.	*Lift chest high to view out rather than lowering head down. Push down with hands on surface.*	Firm client's heels to ground. Firm hands to surface. Stand to side, place palm at upper back, and forearm or sandbag at blanketed low back.
5. Chair Sit *Inviting Wisdom Adhi Mudra,* hands to heart, or other intuitive hand-placement.	Sit quietly. Or guide through RAIN: See tarabrach.com for the *RAIN technique.*	*Recognize. Allow. Inquire. Nourish.* Eyes softly open during inquiry. Choose visual or inspirational focal point.	Guide RAIN meditation, offering opportunities to speak throughout and afterward. *Listen.*

SUMMARY OF FINDINGS

Lesson 1. *Move toward the midline.*
Respect physical and mental constriction as you would the cell fabric that becomes a scab. Do not expand outward. Strengthen inward, direction of the tender weave.

Lesson 2. *Tailor but guide.*
The bodies of many assault survivors will hold physical recall of the event in detail that surpasses cognitive awareness or verbal capacity. Tailor to the individual but guide with the ten anchors (see: *Elements of Practice*). Usual practices may not generate safety at this time.

Lesson 3. *Observe with care.*
Knowing one trigger does not exempt the assault survivor from experiencing new ones. Triggers can be more potent than the initial trauma. Observe sensations and practice in a supportive environment.

Lesson 4. *Call upon wisdom.*
The sheaths, or *koshas*, are disrupted by an assault. Do not emphasize breathing practices. Put minimal strain on executive function. Do not seek bliss. Call on deep knowing for courage and guidance. *Vijnanamaya kosha*, the wisdom sheath, is key.

Lesson 5. *Root to rise.*
Strong, physically and mentally anchoring practices give rise to the breath and promote the wisdom sheath.

Lesson 6. *Meaningful Action breeds health.*
Each productive, meaningful action creates purpose and connection between self and world, and registers as improved well-being.

REFERENCES

1. Acierno, R., Resnick, H.S., et al. (2003) An acute post-rape intervention to prevent substance use and abuse. *Addictive Behaviors 28: 1701–1715.*

2. Ackerman, D. (2004). *An Alchemy of Mind.* New York, NY: Scribner. pp. 105–110.

3. Brach, T. (2013) *Working with Difficulties: The Blessings of RAIN.* tarabrach.com

4. Brooks, David, (2014) The Art of Presence, *NY Times,* Jan 20, 2014.

5. Brown, S.L., Brown, R.M. (2015) Connecting prosocial behavior to improved physical health: Contributions from the neurobiology of parenting. *Neuroscience & Biobehavioral Reviews Apr 20;55:1–17.*

6. Chaitow, L., Gilbert, C., Morrison, D. (2013) *Recognizing and Treating Breathing Disorders: A Multidisciplinary Approach,* Churchill Livingstone.

7. Burrows, C.J. (2011) Acceptance and commitment therapy with survivors of adult sexual assault: a case study. *Clinical Case Studies Journal 12(3):246–259.*

8. Chan, C.L., Chan, T.H., Ng, S.M. (2006). The strength-focused and meaning-oriented approach to resilience and transformation (SMART): A body-mind-spirit approach to trauma management. *Social Work Health Care 43(2–3):* *9–36.*

9. Chen, Y., Lyga, J. (2014) Brain-skin connection: stress, inflammation and skin aging. *Inflammation & Allergy – Drug Targets Journal 13(3):177–190.*

10. Gard, T., Noggle, J.J., Park, C.L., Vago, D.R., Wilson, A. (2014) Potential self-regulatory mechanisms of yoga for psychological health. *Frontiers in Human Neuroscience. 8:770*

11. Jamieson, J.P., Nock, M.K., Mendes, W.B. (2012) Mind over matter: Reappraising arousal improves cardiovascular and cognitive responses to stress. *Journal of Experimental Psychology: General 141(3): 417–422.*

12. Keller, A., Litzelman, K., Witt, W.P. (2012). Does the perception that stress affects health matter? The association with health and mortality. *Healthy Psychology 31(5): 677–684.*

13. Lasater, J. (1995) *Relax and Renew.* Berkeley, CA: Rodmell Press.

14. Le Page, J. and L. (2013). *Mudras for Healing and Trans-formation,* Integrative Yoga Therapy.

15. Litz, B., Gray, M., Bryant, R., Adler, A. (2002) Early intervention for trauma: current status and future directions. *Clinical Psychology 9(2):112-134 (also found at the National Center for PTSD, U.S. Department of Veterans Affairs).*

16. Mason, H., Ugargol, V. (2014) *Mental Health & Mind Body Science,* London: The Minded Institute.

17. McGonigal, K. (2013). *How to Make Stress Your friend.* TEDGlobal.

18. Percy, J. (2015, February 22). The Wake of Grief, *The New York Times Book Review,* review of *The Evil Hours* by David Morris; citing trauma scholar Jonathan Shay, p.18.

19. Porges, S. (2013) *How the Brain Works — Is the Brain Wired for Empathy?* Interview, National Institute for the Clinical Application of Behavioral Medicine, https://www.nicabm.com/how-the-brain-works-with-the-vagus-empathy-and-more

20. Porges, S. (2011). *The Polyvagal Theory,* Norton, New York.

21. Poulin, M.J., Brown, S.L., Smith, D.M. (2013). Giving to others and the association between stress and mortality. *American Journal of Public Health 103(9), 1649–1655.*

22. Qin, J.F., Jin, F.G., Quan, H., Ian, I., Ni, H., Wang, Y. (2015) Adrenergic receptor b2 activation by stress promotes breast cancer progression through macrophages M2 Polarization promoting tumor microenvironment. *BMB Reports (no page access).*

23. Stages of recovery: "Dealing with Trauma of Sexual Assault" (2020) from *The Sex Abuse Treatment Center, Hawaii.* satchawaii.com/get-help/dealing-with-trauma-of-sexual-assault/

24. Sherin, J.E., Nemeroff, C.B. (2011) Post-traumatic stress disorder: the neurobiological impact of psychological trauma. *Journal of Neuroscience 13(3): 263–278.*

25. Smith, S.M., Vale, W.W. (2006) The role of the hypothalamus-pituitary-adrenal axis in neuroendocrine responses to stress. *NIH, Dialogues Clin Neurosci: Dec 8: 383–395.*

26. Streeter, C.C., Gerberg, P.L., Saper, R.B. Ciraulo, D.A., Brown, R.P. (2012) Effects of yoga on the autonomic nervous system, gamma-aminobutyric-acid, and allostasis in epilepsy, depression, and post-traumatic stress disorder. *Medical Hypotheses 10:1016.*

27. Uvnas-Moberg, K., Petersson, M. (2005) Oxytocin, a mediator of anti-stress, well-being, social interaction, growth and healing. *Z Psychosom Med Psychother. 51(1): 57–80.*

28. Zoellner, L.A., Feeny, N.C., Foa, E.B. (2011) Changes in negative beliefs following three brief programs for facilitating recovery after assault. *Journal of Depression and Anxiety 28(7):532–540.*

APPENDIX III

NEVER, F-ING-NEVER-AGAIN, LAND

We took it by the throat.
Violated the violation.
After two anniversaries leaving the house
on Hallowe'en

– memories of the police assault in our backyard way too
graphic –

we changed it up. I said,
This year we can either
get out of here
or we can fuck it up with love.

I'll do whatever you want, he said.

Let's take it by the throat, I said and I
dressed as Peter Pan with his guidance:

You have to wear green leggings, he said.

Wendy Bonvechio's leaves of glass
– $1 at her garage sale –
circled my head, a vine of glitter.
And my 6'3", 230 lb. husband

was Tinkerbell.

We made a lot of trick-or-treaters
happy. Especially five girls dressed as
Peter, Wendy, Tinkerbell, and the
Lost Boys.

I called my husband
outside, he
lit on the landing above us

with translucent butterfly wings,
pink and silver angel tiara
offsetting the greying beard, the sparkle of
eyeglasses, the purple chintz see-through fabric
tight-wrapped around men's size 44 cargo shorts –

and the galumphing size 13E shoes with black socks
making it hard, but not impossible, to take flight –

he jingled his bracelet of bells.

It took three years, I'll mention.
I didn't try to work at all this day: I didn't teach,
I didn't write or edit chapters of my book
about the five women I met that night
in the jail cell – I didn't want to remember.

This day I walked in the sun,
I played my blue ukulele, I cleaned the kitchen.
And I sang, in a voice Tinkerbell said he'd missed,

I know a place where dreams are borne.

Diana Tokaji
Hallowe'en 2017

APPENDIX IV

Prompts for

BOOK CLUBS / DISCUSSION GROUPS

1. PATHOS. Which of the six women do you most identify with? Why? What speaks to you about her or her circumstance?

2. TRAPS. What traps show up for the six women in this book? How are these traps formed within the individual, and how are they formed from external influences and oppressions? Are there ways out? Is surrender valid? What traps have you found yourself in? What tools have you used to free yourself or help others?

3. RAGE. Rage and outrage show up in this book. Is rage something you've felt? Are you comfortable or uncomfortable with rage? When is outrage a useful, motivating emotion, and when do you find it destructive? How do you channel rage or recommend it be channeled? Discuss how rage/outrage show up for Baby in relation to the girl(s) who bullied her, and how it surfaces in the narrator's marriage.

4. POLICE. The narrator doesn't fit a profile that reveals racism as the source of the police officers' behavior. Discuss how U.S. law enforcement's history underlies policing today, and how that shows up (or doesn't) in interactions experienced by you, your loved ones, or as witnessed in current events. What points touch you personally as the narrator shows her process and the effects of a police assault? What were points of irritation?

5. STRANGERS. The narrator finds herself in a cell with women who are strangers to her and about whom she knows nothing—except that they have been arrested for alleged crimes. Discuss what struck you about this circumstance and how the women felt their way through it. Have you found yourself in an intimate circumstance with a stranger or strangers, and if so, how did that work out?

6. SANITY. The topic of sanity and craziness surface intermittently throughout the book, both in the cell and outside the cell, for example, after the narrator leaves Progress Place, having been turned away from serving there. We have a lot of judgments about what is sane behavior, what is insane. In the cell, how was the sanity line clear and how was it blurred? Have there been times you felt isolated or crazy or afraid you were losing your grip on mental health? Have there been times when by "de-pathologizing" the situation, you normalized your (or another's) response and reframed it as reasonable or even healthy?

7. TOOLS. The narrator uses various tools to survive this assault and the aftermath. Name one or more that stood out to you and share why. What tools did she *not* use that you would have chosen or recommended? Discuss tools you've used in the past that were key to surviving a tough circumstance.

8. LOVE AND HATE. There's a lot about struggle in this book—the plights of all the women and the narrator's many challenges are real. But there's also a lot of love. Talk about where you were reminded of humanity in its destructive forms, and where you were reminded of our deep connections: spoken, sensory, or of the spirit.

ABOUT THE AUTHOR

Diana Tokaji, MSc, C-IAYT, is a writer, choreographer, and certified yoga therapist. Winner of the 2020 Sonia Sanchez-Langston Hughes Poetry Contest awarded by Split This Rock, she has published in feminist presses, parenting magazines, anthologies, newspapers, and literary reviews including Bellevue Literary, Author, Tiferet, and The New Guard (2019 finalist). Her first book, *SURVIVING ASSAULT: Words that Rock & Quiet & Tell the Truth—Resource for the Living*, is an intimate conversation directed to survivors of personal or collective trauma. Ms. Tokaji's celebrated blend of spoken word and dance has been featured in London, San Francisco, and Washington, D.C., where her Capital Fringe Festival productions were voted Pick of the Fringe. A twice-certified yoga therapist, she offers private sessions and professional workshops for women: her strength-focused protocol for acute trauma care was honored by Maryland University of Integrative Health for "service and dedication to the community...and the larger world." Forthcoming in 2021 please find her collected works, *Book of Essays Before I Die*.

DianaTokaji.com

LAST WORD

The author would like to acknowledge divinity that comes in many forms of savior and wisdom—and as human, too. One desperate example was the night when video footage showed the shooting of Ahmaud Arbery. This graphic death hit amidst pandemic, job loss, death of loved ones, and the myriad destructive acts by our nation's head bully.

Personally, I'd just returned to this manuscript, and was struggling already to keep my spirits up. The video of that shooting triggered renewed muteness and the same isolation I'd felt after my own assault. I sat up in bed the entire night. Sobbed for our country; gestured hissing snakes of rage; released physically what I had not one word for. And when I was spent, I realized sorrowfully, that I did not have the strength during our collective crisis to publish this story. I could claw at every horror and every unheard abuse, beg them to disappear. But the reoccurrences showed the truth that they will not. I would have to quit the book project, retire it to the file. I wasn't strong enough to withstand this much snuffed light.

Or, maybe if I could create an infrastructure that existed inside this very story, *it* could midwife the book. Maybe if I could be in safe space with five other women, together in a *contrasting* idea of a Cell –not as prison, but "cell" as modicum of life, that which is both *organism and building block of all organisms*— maybe then I could muster the strength to speak. I look up the word "cell" for the first time, and find it derives from the Latin *cella*, or "small room"...*the smallest unit of life.* Six Women in a Cell would go down, or it would demand a *cell*, a basic, structural, functional, and biological unit of six women to survive— to backbone me while I birth it with the book designer's skilled hands. I wrote up a list of women who are powerful and compassionate, who invoke the Michele Obama's of the world but are more within my reach--authors, speakers, activists, holistic health practitioners, leaders, teachers: *Maddie Brennan, Anne Esguerra, Kirsten Pullin, Lisa Schamess, Dawn Valentine, Cinema Wood.* They came into the cell and helped me deliver.

ALSO BY DIANA TOKAJI:

SURVIVING ASSAULT:
Words that Rock & Quiet & Tell the Truth
Resource for the Living

Available at Amazon and at Politics and Prose Bookstore

Surviving an assault to heart, mind, or body
takes will and courage.

4 Conversations. 4 Supportive Hand Mudra.

"This book is a beautiful light for anyone stumbling with darkness."

CPSIA information can be obtained
at www.ICGtesting.com
Printed in the USA
LVHW030925301120
672995LV00002B/85

9 781734 148510